Made with Love

St. Martin's Paperbacks Titles
by Elizabeth Peace Zipern

COOKING WITH THE DEAD

MADE WITH LOVE

Made with Love

Elizabeth Peace Zipern

ST. MARTIN'S PAPERBACKS

This book has not been sponsored or endorsed in any way by the Grateful Dead.

A portion of this book's proceeds will be donated to the Rex Foundation.

MADE WITH LOVE

Copyright © 1996 by Elizabeth Zipern.

All photographs printed by Mark Dabelstein.

Chapter-opener illustrations by Raquel Heiny.

ISBN: 0-312-95800-5

Printed in the United States of America

St. Martin's Paperbacks edition/August 1996

10 9 8 7 6 5 4 3 2 1

For everyone with a little Dead in their hearts. . .
And to the Grateful Dead, for thirty years of bliss and joy.

❀ Contents ❀

The Scene–Highgate, Vermont. Photo: Mark Dabelstein

❀

✿ Introduction ✿

. . . and this is life
green and sprouting
set in its hues
loving the shape of each crack in the wood
flowing bursts of sunlight
opposite a full harvest moon
walls, speckled and illuminated
always in these circles . . .
         —E. ZIPERN

It is July 9, 1995, and the floor of Chicago's Soldier Field is rumbling and roaring with the ecstatic cheers of thousands of fans clapping for more. The Grateful Dead's first double encore in many years is ending, and taking over the stage are steady blasts of screeching and writhing waves of electric guitar. The instrument sings and ripples in tune with the thunderous explosions of fireworks and smoke ripping through the smoggy sky above. Nothing left to do but stand in awe. Summer tour is over.

Colors swirl in and out of embraces. Everyone is soaking in the collective vibes of the Grateful Dead and the tremendous energy the band has graciously extended to their fans of thirty sometimes strange, sometimes long, but always celebratory, years.

Leaving the stadium, smoke and fading fireworks still light up the sky. A feeling of finality. Amazement. The end. It shakes the seats. The show is over.

Masses hurry out into the parking lot bazaar to carry on the night's activities while the encore's lyrics resonate in the air. I will walk alone . . . sing me a song of my own . . . Was the show really over? Had the Dead really encored with two songs? Was it as intense for everyone else too? Is this the end, or just the beginning? Questions left unanswered, good-byes uttered quickly, addresses written on bits of paper, discarded or planned for next time. Next tour . . .

Thirty-one days later, an entire new reality opened. On August 9, Jerry Garcia, longtime demigod and father figure in the ultimate heart-of-gold band, died.

Time has passed, and the emotions, thoughts and feelings surrounding the death of the much-revered musician are still being compiled. To celebrate his life and to pass on the light is now the focus.

Jerry Garcia and the Grateful Dead's music created a better meaning for our existence. It jolted us with the actuality of life's magic and energy and gave us inspiration along the way. Listening to the soulful, passionate notes flowing from Jerry's guitar, we were ultimately struck with the joy of being alive, conscious and awake. We miss him dearly.

The Grateful Dead's plan was to crash through into the millennium, a feat of epic proportions— the longest-touring band in rock history. Not all things end the way they should, or as we had hoped, but for a long time and through a lot of souls, the Dead have existed as a stepping stone into something more. They provided us the opportunity to open vast doorways into discovery, other levels of consciousness and into expanded thought. Alongside them, we saw there was a realm beyond the paramount reality set before us. We saw that we could be more than we ever thought possible. We found that we truly are the eyes of the world.

Through the Grateful Dead we learned about one another and ourselves. On tour, we were thrust into situations, some wonderful and some just plain weird. We were asked to learn, grow, focus, to be alive and above all, to be happy.

For thirty years, the Grateful Dead scene has fed a thriving culture of its own, a lifestyle like no other. The psychedelic legacy which has trailed them permeates so many segments of American society.

This second collection of parking-lot creations and stories is an offering to remember. It is to recall and record the sounds, colors, thoughts, feelings and ideas on the last Grateful Dead tour.

As was the first attempt at capturing this fantastic world on paper, this book is a peek into the wide world of Grateful Dead parking lots as seen through food. One glance into these lots and it was clear: Deadheads will always celebrate life together.

Made with Love goes on tour and takes a trip into these parking lots over eight months of the Dead's last three tours, beginning in the eclectic but always energizing parking lots of the Oakland Coliseum in the winter of 1994 and ending with the last show of the 1995 summer tour in Chicago.

Over the years, the parking lot, and its marketplace atmosphere, has transcended the boundaries of the venues that have held them. Grateful Dead parking lot–inspired arts and crafts are popping up everywhere. A chapter of these items is included to showcase the beautiful things Deadheads create. It is my hope they will inspire and illustrate what we can achieve on our own.

To decipher many of the ingredients, a glossary is included to familiarize the reader with foods found in natural-food stores and co-ops. I urge everyone to check these places out. Never will you find such an assortment of whole, healthy, pesticide-free food in one place.

Please keep in mind while reading that Jerry Garcia's departure from this earth is seldom mentioned, for most of the events occurred before August 9, 1995. Thoughts and remembrances on his life, death and the impact on the future of the Grateful Dead are included by vendors who were reinterviewed.

Hope it all reminds you . . .

Elizabeth Peace Zipern
Tucson, Arizona
October 1995

Any Day Soups

Hanging out in the parking lot with Carla Odenheim is like spending time with an old friend. Sipping a mixed drink concoction, she'll laugh and tell you how she once bumped into her brother, Erich, by almost getting run off of the road by him (he's a truck driver) while traveling through Colorado. Or maybe she'll tell you how much she loves the Grateful Dead, the beautiful people who go to Dead shows, or the yummy soups she loves to make.

"I make a pretty good ass mushroom stew," she'll exclaim. "It looks like hell, but it tastes pretty good."

Carla hasn't made soup for any members of the Grateful Dead, yet, but she has waited on some of them while working at a restaurant in San Francisco.

"Not that long ago, before a Rolling Stones concert, Phil and Bobby came in with a bunch of other people," she explains. "They all ate the same thing, veggie calzones. Nine of them. I waited on them, and I was freaking out. I said to them, 'I really appreciate the music, and . . . how was your calzone?' It was the most I could say." She laughs. "My hand was totally shaking. I was like, 'Ohmigod, I'm going to drop the calzone on this guy.' It was so cool, it was such a rush."

Since 1992 Carla has been going to and cooking at Dead shows. Living and working in the Dead community has enriched her life with friends, music and food; a sharp contrast from living in New Jersey and working in the financial community.

Carla (Vegan Bean Soup). Photo: Mark Dabelstein

"In my former life, I was a stockbroker," Carla relates. "I decided that nine to five wasn't for me. I said, 'I hate this place, I hate New Jersey, I hate offices, I want to go and be free and travel and have fun.' I just said, 'Screw it!' and I picked up and moved to Albuquerque and from there started hanging out with cool people and started saying, 'You know, there is a lot more to life than making money.'"

Carla's "Not for Nuthin'" Yummy Vegan Bean Soup
* Makes 14 Fat Servings *

* Needed—a 2 to 3 quart pot.
* Hints from the chef —When Carla cooks, she tries to make her dishes as easy as possible, so look at what you have in the fridge and use what you can.
* Substitute fresh ingredients for canned whenever you can.

1 Tb. olive oil

At least 6 cloves garlic, minced ("It ain't worth making it if it doesn't have garlic," she says.)

2 "fat" onions, minced

15 oz. bean soup mix (this packaged mixture of beans for soup can be found in stores) or use 15 oz. of any other favorite beans, soaked and cooked

1 cube vegetable bouillon

2 15 oz. cans vegetable broth (or make your own stock—see following recipe)

2 15 oz. cans peeled tomatoes

3 celery stalks, diced

2 russet potatoes, peeled and cubed

3 to 4 carrots, sliced

Lots of mushrooms, sliced ("Add if you like them and you have the cash," says Carla.)

Fresh-ground black pepper, salt or soy sauce, cayenne, garlic powder, all to taste

Rosemary, thyme, 2-3 bay leaves, dill, parsley, sage, to taste

21 seasoning generic spice ("It's always good to add because it has everything in it," says Carla.)

• In a pot, saute the garlic and onions in olive oil. After they soften, add the cooked beans and continue to saute.

• Now, fill the pot with 2 to 3 cups of water. Add the bouillon, vegetable broth, peeled tomatoes. (Squish the tomatoes with your hands—extremely fun to do.) Now, throw in the celery stalks, potatoes, carrots and mushrooms.

• Once it gets cookin', herb it. "Herb what you have, herb what you can get fresh," says Carla. "I've got a rosemary bush in front of my house, so I herb it with rosemary. Somebody gave me some fresh sage, so one day I herbed it with sage. Take a big whole, fat clump of fresh parsley, mince it up and throw it in. Do what you can, use what you've got. Improvise!" Add rosemary, thyme, bay leaves, dill, parsley, sage, fresh black pepper, salt or soy sauce, cayenne, garlic powder, and 21 seasoning generic spice.

• Let the soup cook down and stew together on a simmer. Carla recommends serving her soup with a good bagel. When it tastes right, eat! Yummy stuff!

An incessant cook, Carla is always looking for new, creative dishes to make at Dead shows. To warm everyone in the parking lots of the 1994 Oakland Coliseum winter shows, Carla whipped up a batch of Yummy Vegan Bean soup, a longtime favorite.

"I've been to shows and have done the grilled cheese scene," she says. "Everyone does grilled cheese, so I wanted to do something different. Everybody has always really loved my soups. I also make matzo ball soup for the token Jew in everybody. It's made with love."

These days, Carla lives in Berkeley, California, and waitresses at a well-known San Francisco restaurant. She plans on going to culinary school and then opening a vegan and vegetarian restaurant in the Bay area, all of which will give others the opportunity to try her favorite soups.

"I do soups best, but I love to make anything," she proclaims. "I get off on people really enjoying food. I like to see that. Seeing people enjoy what they're eating and just savor every bite, and say, 'This was made with love . . . yeah! Right on! It's good for me!' "

Sumptuous Soup Stock

Stock is used to liven up sauces, stir-fries, soups, whatever. It can be added into any recipe to replace water. This stock will taste wonderful with Carla's Vegan Bean Soup. Carla also recommends having stock around if you're sick. The broth is soothing to drink.

* Use any vegetable, but not cabbage or cauliflower because they'll make the stock bitter.

• In a big pot, take whatever tired veggies you have lying around. "Not spoiled, just tired and poopy," she says. Perhaps a few onions, crush some garlic cloves (crack them with the flat of a knife). "Chop a few carrots in half. Quarter and core an apple or pear, throw in some celery, a few tomatoes, some quartered potatoes, a turnip is always very good, a handful or so of whole peppercorns," adds Carla. "Also some tamari, a bay leaf, fresh parsley and a basil leaf or two."
• Add about 2 or 3 quarts of water. This shouldn't be strongly flavored, it is a stock, not a soup. Cook it all down, then strain and compost the vegetables if you can. All the goodness is gone, so enrich your soil by composting with it.
• Freeze and use whenever you need it.

* See Carla's Veggie Pot Stickers recipe in the Decadent and Delectable Main Dishes chapter.

His vending space is an intersection, the corner of a back road that connects to a wider, more hectic Shakedown packed with people. Two blocks over, Pearl Street, the road in front of the Knickerbocker Arena, looks as if it has been taken over by floods of tie-dye.

Every local vendor has trekked to the downtown Albany, New York, streets for the occasion. As a result, the Lot is inundated with vendors, a fact that makes the usual tour vendors a little uneasy about selling everything they've lugged into the parking lot.

Greg, too, is having some trouble selling the soup he has stored in his red Radio Flyer wagon. Greg knows that the soup does much better on spring and fall tours or at night when the temperature cools down outside, but he hangs at his little corner anyway. Even if he doesn't sell anything, the area he and his girlfriend, Marhia, have set up on the curb serves as a home base, a place to rest and wait for the show to begin.

Greg began cooking on tour two years ago when he got clean. Cooking in the Lot gives him a place to land and concentrate. Inside the show, the Wharf Rat community offers him support, and a place to congregate and talk.

"We have something else in common besides the Dead," he says of the Wharf Rats. "We're in a place that traditionally is a very dangerous environment to try and stay clean in. It's nice to be able to see somebody else that's trying to do the same thing and it offers a lot of support. Every show I go to now, I know that there is going to be at least forty people at the Wharf Rat meeting that are going through the exact same things. This will be my twenty-sixth show clean tonight. That says a great statement for the band, that it's not just about partying, but music is strong enough to endure even beyond that. The music is still as great to me and I get caught in the groove and I jam just as hard now as I ever did when I was using. It's been a real awakening for me. It's not all about the parking lot scene; what it's really about is what goes on inside there, and that's why being out here without a ticket would be real hard for me to deal with. To me, the bottom line has always been the show. If I can't make the show, then I can't make the scene.

"I've never had an official count of how many shows I've done, but I'm going to be over one hundred by the end of this tour, so I've gone to one hundred shows and have never gone without a ticket. It would break my heart to be here without a ticket, hoping to be miracled in and knowing that the band is starting up. That would drive me nuts. In fact, I've never been outside while they're playing."

Almost ten years after his first Dead show in 1975, Greg learned to avoid the hassles of professional ticket organizations, scalpers and other problems by ordering tickets through the Grateful Dead Ticket Service, also known as mail order. GDTS gives everyone an opportunity to buy tickets and a fair chance for a good seat.

"I guess it was '81 that I went to my first out of state shows and multiple shows and from then on I started doing as many shows a year that I could financially and responsibly manage," recalls Greg. "In 1983 somebody showed me mail order. They gave me a ticket to the Alpine Valley shows. It was a mail-order ticket, with the glitter ink and stuff, and I was just like, 'Wow, how do you get these?' In '85 I started mail ordering for all the shows, and I've been mail ordering ever since. Even though they have always said that it's a first come, first serve basis, it seems like tickets have gotten better over the years. It seems like every tour where I've mail ordered multiple cities, I get at least one ticket that's within the first twenty rows. In the past couple of years, I usually mail order two tickets at a time and miracle somebody.

"One of the shows they're doing this year is a Rex Foundation show and I'm really excited about that," claims Greg. "I saw a thing on public TV that explained the Rex stuff and it talked about Phil's part, where he gives a twelve thousand dollar grant to these struggling composers that the mainstream won't accept and they don't have the funds to get studio time. They give them this grant so they can rent a studio and get their music recorded. You just don't hear of other bands out there doing that.

Greg's Homemade Veggie Soup
Serves 10

1 Tb. olive oil (enough to lightly cover the bottom of the pot)
1/2 med. head of red cabbage, cubed
6 large new potatoes, cubed large
3 large carrots, sliced round
3 large celery stalks, sliced horizontally
1/4 pound fresh green beans
1 15 oz. can sweet corn
1 15 oz. can diced tomatoes
2 quarts tomato or vegetable juice
1/4 cup chopped onions
1 Tb. black pepper
1 Tb. salt
Hot and spicy seasoning (sprinkle enough to cover the surface—will be spicy)

• Heat a 1 1/2 to 2 gallon pot and add olive oil. Add all the ingredients except the onions and spices and bring to a boil for half an hour. Then, add the onions, black pepper, salt and seasoning mix.
• Simmer for 6 to 8 hours. (Greg says the green beans and carrots take the longest to cook.) Remove from heat, cover and let sit until the pot is cool enough to pick up with your hands.
• Freeze, refrigerate or serve. The spices will be more flavorful and the vegetables will hold together better after sitting a day.

"My favorite bootlegs are still the ones from the sixties when Pig Pen was around, when they would get up and play just for the hell of it. Now, it has evolved into such an interaction between the guys in the band. The chemistry between Jerry, Bob and Phil, it's like each one knows where the other one is going at any given time and that gives them the freedom to play their own stuff. When they get up there and they get into a jam, there's nobody on earth that could touch what they do with music, there's nobody else that approaches music with that attitude, that the song is just a framework to build around. The music supersedes the written notes that goes into a feeling. I've always believed that special things really happen when they're on stage and even on their worst nights, they still have those moments where Jerry comes through and it's just that pure Grateful Dead sound that nobody can match. When I'm sitting idle with music running through my head, it's usually their music. That's a statement in itself.

"Even my best bootlegs can't match what it sounds like live. The way Phil's bass rolls off the stage and you can feel it in your lungs when he's playing. There's nobody else that plays like that, he plays lead bass the whole show, he's out there for three hours a night, it just blows me away. Over the years he's the one that has really done even more than Jerry and Bobby. Phil has really gotten into the music inside me. There's nothing like the way Phil Lesh plays bass, it's amazing. When I have a chance to get close near his speakers, those are the shows that I still have the most powerful memories of."

A few hours after it had officially opened, Dan, Stacey and their friends Sunshine, Shiro, Katie and Nikki sauntered into the parking lot of the Los Angeles Sports Arena for the second night of the Dead's 1994 run. Once in the Lot, the six set out to find friends, tickets and to relax, since the show was still hours away.

Dan has always loved the idea of providing food for people. A free kitchen. Common at Rainbow Gatherings and in the parking lots of Dead shows, free kitchens begin when a gatherer collects food to cook for everyone. So in his big pot, Dan collected a mix of ingredients and set out to cook for the communal benefit of all in the parking lot of the Grateful Dead. He called it Shakedown Sopa.

"I had a bunch of canned tomatoes and tomato sauce, and that was about it," says Dan. "When we got here I was talking with some people and telling them that I wanted to make a big pot of stew or something. Some people gave me potatoes and rice, and they just said, 'Spread the word.' We also met up with our friend and she brought over this whole box full of

Dan (Shakedown Sopa). Photo: E. Zipern

potatoes. Other people gave us salad, jicama and let us use their can opener. Everyone helped out slicing carrots and potatoes. The only thing that kinda sucked was that it took the entire show to make it. It wasn't really done until everybody was starting to leave the Lot!"

Dan grew up eating, cooking and smelling the wonderful aromas from the Sopa his mom made when he was young. He would help her by cutting vegetables and mixing the ingredients.

"My mom used to make it when I was really little and I was just always watching her cook," remembers Dans. "When I moved out, I always wanted to make it for myself. One time I was putting pepper in, and the top came off, and almost the entire jar of pepper went in. We ate it anyway. It tasted so good, but we were sweating balls, dude," he says, laughing.

Dan has been a Dead devotee since 1986 but didn't start going into the shows steadily until 1992. "That's when they really blew me away," he recalls. "When I saw them, I thought it was the most incredible thing I'd ever seen.

"I love it here so much." He smiles and grins, almost at the same time. "I can wear a skirt, and no one questions it. It's such a relief from society. I try to describe it to people, so I say, 'It's just like a big flea market. You can find most anything you've ever wanted here.' I've seen really cool art, pictures, everything!

"People have such a misinterpretation of what it's all about. They think it's strictly drugs. People here are so nice. I can go and hug a brother, and it's cool. Just hug a bunch of people. It's so weird how people in regular

Shakedown Sopa (Soup)
Serves as many people as you have ingredients!
(Probably around 6)

"This is the way I make it at my house," says Dan. "I tried to make it here that way, but it didn't quite come out. It still tastes pretty good though."

Dan says an exact recipe does not necessarily need to be followed. Combine whatever you have and create your own delicious soup.

5 cups water
Assorted vegetables (or meat) for stock (roasted and peeled green chiles are highly recommended)
3 carrots, sliced
1 potato, diced small
1 cup cooked noodles or 1 cup rice (browned, but not cooked), your choice
1 15 oz. can tomato sauce, stewed tomatoes or diced tomatoes
Juice of 1/2 lemon
1 or 2 brown or red chiles, minced
Salt, pepper and garlic salt, to taste

• In a large pot, make a stock by adding assorted vegetables or meat to boiling water. "If you like chicken or meat, put that in first, then you get the juice from whatever you're boiling into the water," explains Dan. "You can do this with vegetables. I usually make it with beef or chicken."
• Add the carrots and potato. Let cook for 10 minutes to soften, then add the rice or cooked noodles. If using rice, do not cook first. Simply brown it by quickly sauteing in a few tablespoons of oil, stirring constantly. Add to the soup.
• Next, add the tomato sauce, lemon and minced chiles. To taste, add the salt, pepper and garlic salt.
• Let simmer and continue adding water if necessary. Feel free to add other favorite spices. Fresh or dried dill weed also tastes great.

9

society don't see that. Kinda strange. People at work trip out on me because I'm happy and nice all the time. They're just like, 'What are you so happy about?'"

The three Los Angeles shows gave Dan a taste of touring again. The weekend was a reminder of how he loves to spend his time—on tour with the Dead. For Dan, the decision to stop working at a local drugstore in California or to go on tour is a constant dilemma. Like so many Deadheads, the itch to get out on the road is eventually too hard to ignore.

"I've just been confused because I want to go on tour bad, but there are so many things holding me back and there are so many things telling me to go. It's a major battle in my head. And I love 'em too much just to completely stop going.

"The Dead are really cool," he continues. "Everything about them, the way they change. They're just like every band in one. They can groove, they can rock, they can make you cry. I've sat there in my van and cried. I love them so much. It's the weirdest feeling. I don't know why. I was in there last night going, 'Why do I love them so much?' It kinda tears me apart a little bit. I feel so much in there. I wonder so much about what they are thinking about. I sense a respect between them and the audience, and I just wonder sometimes."

Various Liquids

❀ ❤ ❀

It is the last night of the 1995 summer tour at Soldier Field in Chicago, and with a tour full of early morning espresso and iced mochas behind them, Rob and Audrey are tired. After much consideration, the couple has decided against selling their tickets to the show, although they could use a nap. They have spent all day, and the entire tour for that matter, feeding everybody's coffee jones from the back of their blue-gray Volkswagen bus.

For the majority of the Dead's 1995 East and West Coast summer tour, Rob and Audrey have offered many of the usual drinks that one would find in a cafe. The only espresso vendors on the lot, by early every morning, the couple found themselves swamped by vendors and others who had tracked them, desperate for their caffeine fix.

"If we stayed the night in the Lot, it was as soon as they woke up. We had people ready for coffee as we were lining up, waiting to get in the Lot," says Audrey. "And then as soon as we were in the Lot, all the other vendors would be at our van, waiting for us, standing around going, 'When is the van going to be ready, when can we have coffee?'

"After like three o'clock in the morning, pulling massive espresso shots for the past two hours, you can't even remember the time going by because it has been so crazy and busy.

Audrey and Rob (Iced Double Mocha). Photo: Mark Dabelstein

We were exhausted but it was still good; it was a good exhaustion. People were definitely appreciative, and that made me feel good. I really enjoyed giving people what they wanted."

The plan to create a traveling espresso shop arose when Rob and a friend came up with the idea of offering espresso on the Lot. After Rob and Audrey were married, they invested in an espresso machine and went to work. Rob knew he wanted to start his business in the Dead scene after going to his first show in 1992.

"I went down to the Eugene shows with a bunch of my

12

friends about four years ago," says Rob. "I was like, 'Wow, I really dig this whole scene, this is where it is.' Since then I wanted to be part of touring. But to make it work, you had to support yourself, and the espresso van just happened to fit. Because espresso is nothing more than extremes, and I think the Lot is nothing more than extremes."

Because he was able to work and play in the same atmosphere, Rob found earning a living in the scene to be incredibly satisfying.

> # Iced Double Mocha
> ## *Serves 1*
>
> *Needed—An espresso machine. Home espresso makers are great for this!
>
> 2 1-ounce shots of espresso
> 1 ounce chocolate syrup (they like to use Hershey's)
> 7 ounces milk
>
> Ice, to taste
> Raspberry, mint or any other syrup, optional
>
> • Grind the coffee, pull the shot of espresso, pour it into a glass and add chocolate syrup. Now, add the milk and as much ice as you like to cool.
> • Spice it up by adding flavored syrups.

"I loved it," he says. "That's what I made the business for and that's why I'm a business owner, so I can play and work at the same time, even though it's hard work. Working in the Lot is probably the hardest job I ever had, getting in there every morning and getting to shows and being on time and keeping the van running. It's hard work, but it pays off."

Soon, Rob and Audrey will open a cafe where they can sell books and games, and provide a place for people to study, hang out, drink coffee and eat. They also plan to continue going to "Star Parties"—all-night astronomy affairs where Rob and Audrey provide the caffeine to help people stay up, gazing into the heavens.

"They're a blast," says Audrey. "People go up with monstrously huge telescopes, I mean these are telescopes that I have to stand on a ten-foot ladder just to look inside. I've seen galaxies that are twenty billion light-years away. They have huge telescopes and they go up on a mountain where there's no city lights, and they stay up all night long, looking at stars and galaxies and comets and it's amazing what these people know. We just go up and sell espresso and we get to star gaze and learn so much about the galaxy. They're just incredible.

"At a Star Party, it's a different crowd (than at Dead shows)," says Audrey. "But you still have crazy, wild, intellectual, really fun people who just stand around and love to talk. It's the only job where I've supported myself where I've never been tired of doing it."

It was a hot, sunny, dusty day and many more people were still streaming into the Franklin County Airport, in Highgate, Vermont. The far end of the airport's grassy field was the designated vending area, but the selling, trading and bartering of every item imaginable went on everywhere. The night before, Gillian and her friends whipped up a last-minute batch of Gillian's herbal potion, aptly named Tour Hack Sap. Into small, brown glass bottles, Gillian poured the liquid concentration of herbs; a potion intended to heal and expectorate sick and tired bodies.

Gillian first learned about creating herbal remedies while traveling on Grateful Dead tour. Years of interest in healing began a passion that eventually lead to a two-year intensive course in herbal medicine in California, then on to practicing through her home.

"I started on tour, working with another woman who knew a bit more about herbs than myself and being really curious and pursuing it as far as I could, all the way to the point of searching out schools," says Gillian. "It was burning in me to follow through with it. After the first course, I felt I needed more education to be confident in healing others. So for two years I lived and worked at the school, learning and growing directly with the plants. But it definitely started with hemp, just learning that hemp is an herb and if that is an herb it has some medicinal effect. Now there's two zillion herbs in my head that have a purpose.

Gillian (Tour Hack Sap). Photo: Mark Dabelstein

"Grateful Dead Land is the best place to put out the word on the medicinal properties of herbs and get people focused on taking care of themselves, because I feel like that's lost. The whole Denny's generation, instead of cooking food anymore, it's all fast food, fast life. It's the 'give me a pill to fix it fast' attitude. It's unfortunate how out of touch we've become with our roots."

Gillian has worked hard to create an herbal concoction to heal tired bodies that drive all day and dance to the Dead all night. A part of the Dead community since 1985, Gillian has found that shows are a great place to get the word out on herbal remedies.

"I was fourteen when I started seeing shows and then I started touring when I was sixteen," she explains. "My initial attraction was the vending thing and I always dug on the music. I loved the feeling, the people, the scene, more so than the music. Soon enough, I was really involved in the music and I became addicted to the tunes. I loved it all, so I kept going.

"For me, it wasn't write down set lists, it wasn't count how many shows, it was the

14

Tour Hack Sap

According to Gillian, Tour Hack Sap is an elixir, an all-around healer. "For me, it's a seasonal thing, it changes with the seasons and with the availability of herbs," she says. "There's a couple of basic herbs. Anybody can come up with a formula. I really encourage people to create their own formulas directed to their own bodies."

Herbs can be replaced with whatever is more accessible and also with herbs you are familiar with. Substitutions are up to your discretion. "It's what your body takes to," explains Gillian.

A few words on obtaining herbs. . .
—Always smell and taste to make sure they're fresh
—The herbs should retain somewhat of a color or a vibrance
—Ask questions about where the herbs come from
—Ask how long they've been sitting, what the turnover is, and if they are stored in amber glass
 (Gillian says many herbs are light sensitive)
—Phone books are great (and essential) for finding quality herb shops
—*The Village Herbalist* is a quarterly publication with listings on where to get herbs, finding
 contacts and herbalism schools

INDICATIONS
 For the treatment of bronchial infections, colds, congestion, seasonal allergies and tour hack.

CONTRAINDICATIONS
 Do not use if pregnant or nursing. Consult your physician if you are taking any "evil pharmaceuticals."

DOSAGE
 Take as much as you feel your body needs. Start off with a few tablespoons.
Note—this is a home remedy. If you have any questions, check with a doctor.

BASE
4 onions, minced
1 head garlic, minced
Fresh burdock root, if available (Gillian says this gives the syrup an interesting flavor and it cuts down on the intensity of the garlic taste)
16 ounces unrefined, pure honey

HERBS

✓5 Tbs. rose hips
 5 Tbs. horehound
 4 Tbs. lemon grass
 3 Tbs. yarrow flowers
 3 Tbs. white willow bark
 3 Tbs. mau hung or American ephedra
✓2 Tbs. nettle leaf
 2 Tbs. mullein leaf
✓2 Tbs. echinachea root
 1 Tb. bergamont leaf
✓1 Tb. echinachea leaf

✓1 Tb. red clover
 1 Tb. lungwort
 1 Tb. ginkgo leaf
 1 Tb. lobelia
 1 Tb. elecampane
 1 Tb. Oregon grape root

 2 quarts water
 Amber jars or some other glass container
 Cheesecloth

• First prepare the base. Chop the onions, garlic and the burdock. In a large, nonaluminum pot, steep the onions, garlic and burdock in honey over a low heat for three hours. Stir periodically. Then, strain and cool.
• In another pot, bring the water to a boil and then lower to a low boil. Add the white willow bark, echinachea root, elecampane and Oregon grape root (The bark and roots are heavier herbs. They take a hotter intensity to extract). Boil for 15 minutes, then lower the heat to a simmer.
• Add the rest of the leafs and flowers. Simmer on low for about 10 minutes. Let cool a bit first, then strain through cheesecloth, making sure all the liquid is squeezed out of the herbs.
• To the honey base, add the herb water in a 2-parts herb water to 1-part honey base ratio. Let cool, then bottle in an amber jar (if possible). Refrigeration will make the syrup last longer, but by no means does it need to be kept there.

   For further reading on herbs, Gillian recommends *The New Holistic Herbal* by David Hoffman (Element Books).
   "It's a very well spoken book, easy to follow and to understand. He's a wonderful character too. It's just a good book to start off with."
   This book can be found in the book sections of co-ops or natural food stores. As always, with any book, it can be ordered from a bookstore.
   For more information on herbal programs write or call: Sierra School of Herbs and Health, Dutch Flat, California/P.O. Box 744, Alta, California 95701; 916-389-2554.

moment, definitely the moment. I started making a lot of shows, did this whole school bus thing, then just traveled back and forth across the country. It was the best introduction to the world. I've seen things that you could never see being a tourist, it was like we'd go into towns and we'd become part of that town.

"With the school buses, it would be more of a group consensus. We'd go mining in Arkansas for a couple of weeks, go camping, visit different places, we saw a lot more of the more earth-centered type of tourism. As a tourist, you see mostly highways, but traveling with people who have this certain type of head space, you see more of an earth travel. It was also the feeling of being totally self-sufficient, being able to make money apart from society.

"It was just a free ride across the country, going places with good people who were kind of in the same focus. The music is a strong form, a life force. I believe that about any type of music. It was more about the people and the freedom to shine. I learned so much. It's interesting to see the changes; it's just a reflection of the world, how the whole thing is turning.

"I stopped traveling to focus totally on my herb thing, and it was awesome, though it didn't give me much time to do anything else. On tour, you can live so long, for free, just working, bartering and traveling, riding the tour anywhere and everywhere and getting by. But, you're not really accomplishing much, except for having tons of fun. I guess you're making a statement of sorts. It's a good escape, but there's a lot to do in this world.

"I started to realize all these things that we as human beings need to do, and my niche was with the medicine thing. People need to be helped. This world needs people with a voice and a lot of people with voices are either hiding away in gatherings, hiding from the law, or whatever. People need to come out and become part of society to change society, and that is my main concern. I really want to change society. With my case, it's bringing medicine back to what it was about. Tour is an excellent outlet for me, because there are so many sick people on tour. It's like a reflection, it's getting it out and getting instant feedback because I see a lot of people over and over again. It's a confirmation that the stuff is really good."

Herbal medicine has drawn criticism from mainstream organizations such as the American Medical Association and the Food and Drug Administration. In opposition to these organizational ideologies, Gillian believes the future, or rather, returning to the past, is through herbs.

"The synthetics, chemicals and fillers that make up today's medicine are, for the most part, nonessential, nonefficient and can lead to other problems within the human body," she says.

"It's an issue that's under serious attack right now by the AMA and that's a huge issue. Why wouldn't it be? They would lose a large amount of money and power if we all began to use real medicine again; plants and herbs. Due to their rising demand, herbs are becoming more acknowledged for their properties and are being scientifically proven to be effective.

There was a time in the eighties when herbs were mostly shunned because they were still considered to be used only by a certain 'new ageish' crowd. Today, lots of folks are becoming aware and that's a wonderful thing. Herbs to me are going within yourself and asking yourself what you need, taking responsibility for ourselves. We're programmed to go seek health outwardly when in actuality it's our own bodies and our ailments. This world is so focused on having doctors telling you what to do.

"With herbs it's the real deal, the real thing, it's something we can grow and we can make and we can do ourselves. To take that and to offer it to ourselves and others is what really works, because you're doing something for yourself. I think the reality of doctors is coming on strong, the reality of the medications and the side effects and even the presence of new diseases, the antibiotics that don't cure. We've built up immunities to so many of these medications, it's time to turn back to the earth, we're a part of the earth, we're from the earth, we need to look to the earth to heal.

"The herb thing is something people definitely need to learn and pursue. It's amazing, because once people are into it, and just know the simplest things, their life changes. Because as soon as you start to feel bad, and you eat some raw garlic or take some herbs, it wipes it out before you get sick. I think the lack of information being provided to us as humans is the ability to cure ourselves, the ability to fight off sickness before it develops. . . to be in control of our bodies. Herbs are empowering in the most wonderful way. It's a necessity. All this money is being thrown into health care, but education in self-health care is what needs to come before any more drugs are developed. It's a way that's being ignored, but there's so much to it, and anybody that's into herbs knows it's an amazing thing."

Since she was fifteen, Erin Myers has wanted to go to a Dead show. After two years of convincing her parents, she finally succeeded, and they let her see the 1994 Chicago shows at Soldier Field. Going again the following summer left Erin ecstatic, for the Dead was one of her last favorite bands still touring.

"The first band I got into was the Beatles, their later stuff. I was into the Doors and Deep Purple and I like a lot of folk music," explains Erin. "Then I met Rebecca, and how it started was that we both had a crush on this Deadhead guy who was really cool. Rebecca had already been into the Dead because of her brother. Usually when I'm interested in a person and I think they're a beautiful person, I kind of want to get information on where they're coming from. I just got into it from both of them, and I saw how important it was to Rebecca.

"It was kind of like a mystery, because neither Rebecca or I knew what it would be like, but we knew people who had been there. One thing that I noticed about people who had been to shows or were into the Dead was that they knew how to relax. It was just really intriguing. I was thinking, 'What's the concert going to be like with these people?' It was hard to envision. I did not imagine the dancing, I imagined a bunch of people sitting down in their seats and really, really, listening hard. I didn't imagine the parking lot and it

Herbal Brews

Erin has found that eucalyptus has a calming effect, so she likes to make eucalyptus tea. "It's very soothing to me. It also helps with sinuses that are irritated, especially with allergies. Mint helps congestion," she says.

Erin recommends sprinkling eucalyptus in a bath; or for help with congestion, sprinkle into a bowl of boiling water. Inhale the steam when you have a cold.

Tea bags, a tea strainer, etc. (anything you can put herbs or tea leaves in)
Eucalyptus—this can be found in bulk at most health food stores
Mint leaves—this can be found in bulk at most health food stores
Green tea
Chamomile

- To make the tea, Erin says you won't need a lot of leaves, for a little goes a long way. Add 2 pinches of eucalyptus leaves, each about 1/4 inch thick between your thumb and first finger. For the mint leaves, crumble well before adding into a tea bag or strainer. If you like a strong flavor, use 3 pinches of mint, but 2 will be good for a lightly aromatic flavor.
- Try adding a little green tea or chamomile to the mixture; it will soften the taste.
- Boil water, pour over the eucalyptus and mint leaves and let steep.

Enjoy!

was just amazing to me because I thought there are just going to be a million of these really relaxed, down-to-earth people.

"I think I only assessed what was going on around me for a while and then pretty quickly, I was a part of it. That blew me away because I never felt a part of something so quickly. It was hard to accept.

"I like the diversity within the band, the things that each member has to offer. I love the fact that they've been so many places with so many different people and you can hear it in the music. The music has a universal appeal. It fits in with a lot of different styles. I love that, and it's really relaxing for me, it's like another one of the herbs. I found that throughout high school, with my tea, I'd listen to the Grateful Dead."

Erin (Herbal Brews). Photo: Mark Dabelstein

On the Side

Elizabeth and Michael spent much of their 1995 summer tour cutting, washing and boiling hundreds of pounds of potatoes. In their endeavor to make Cajun style French Fries, at times they spent hours at a show preparing more than two hundred pounds of the spicy, crunchy potato delicacies.

"It's a simple recipe, but it was a lot of work when you're doing two hundred pounds of potatoes, washing, boiling and cutting them all," maintains Elizabeth. "Before we had a slicer in Las Vegas, I did two hundred and fifty pounds of potatoes, sliced them all up myself and I was cramped, it was horrible," she laments. "But then by summer tour we got this awesome slicer, thanks to our friend Dominic. You just put the potato in, pull the lever, and it slices them all!"

Both Michael and Elizabeth's first Dead show was at Deer Creek in '89, although they didn't know each other at the time. Since then, both have spent a significant amount of time on tour and have always come back to Deer Creek, a venue close to their home in Louisville, Kentucky.

"My first show was in Deer Creek in '89, I just kinda went on a whim," explains Michael. "The parking lot experience was pretty interesting, something I had never taken part in. After I got into it a bit, I started drumming, playing hand drums, congas, djembes, and that really attracted me. That was one of the few times that I had had to get together with a community of drummers, and it really got me into some powerful circles. As I got more into it, it was just the community of friends that I was meeting from all over the country.

Elizabeth and Michael (Cajun French Fries). Photo: E. Zipern

"I kinda consider Deer Creek sacred ground. I only missed one show there, and every year I'd go back," he continues. "This summer was terrible, I kinda freaked out when I saw all those people coming over the fence, through the fence and I heard people cheering for it. It left a bad taste in my mouth. I went up to the top, and I was trying to deter people from coming in. They were putting people in jeopardy the way they were coming over—there was just way too much possibility for injury there. It was bad and I knew right when I saw it happening that they would never play Deer Creek again, and that was a terrible feeling."

"When I finally went . . . wow, my mind was blown," recalls Elizabeth. "I thought, this is the most colorful thing ever. I remember thinking the colors were so incredible. There was a Stella Blue that night, and the words touched me, just like they would now. My very first show I was just crying, the whole thing really moved me. Now looking back, knowing what I know, I got a really good first show. After that I was like, 'All right, let's go to more!' I just kept going. I have one hundred and four ticket stubs, and I know I've lost twenty or thirty.

"I think it was a combination of really good music combined with really good energy created from the scene, and I think that's the magic of it all," she says. "Jerry was an incredible guitarist but I think a lot of the magic we all felt was from the energy that we created. The band and the audience, we just created a magic together. We were very much a part of it, sometimes we were a bad part of it," she admits.

Cajun French Fries
Serves 4

10 potatoes, cut in large, thick wedges	2 parts paprika	1 part onion powder
Equal parts canola and corn oil (Mixing half and half will yield a good cooking blend)	1 part cayenne pepper	1 part salt
	1 part white pepper	1/2 part oregano
	1 part black pepper	1/2 part thyme
	1 part garlic powder	

* *Add any other spice you like. The spices are to taste, but the above combination should give you the flexibility to make some really killer fries!*
* *Hot oil splashes easily. Use extreme care when deep-frying.*

• With the skins on, wash the potatoes, then boil them until they're fairly soft on the inside. Let cool, then cut into thick wedges. (The cooling process can be sped up by refrigeration.)
• Deep-fry the potato wedges in the canola-corn oil mix. The oil should be at about 350°, and it's very important that the oil does not burn. Deep-fry quickly so they don't get too greasy. "The idea is to get them hot and crispy and then get them out of there," explains Elizabeth.
• Add the spices together in whatever combinations you like. Pour the mix over the potatoes, mix well and enjoy.

Across the dirt road from the Sam Boyd Stadium in Las Vegas, an unusually large crowd of ticketless stragglers peruse the Shakedown as the Dead move through their second set. The sounds of Drums and then Space thunders from inside the arena, reaching the outer lots with surprising clarity, some beats more vibrant and electrifying than others.

Miranda sits in a flower patterned dress on top of her red cooler, wrapping fresh, sweet corn in tinfoil. Her boyfriend, Tyler, and her eight-month-old dog, a sheperd-husky named Isaac, just left the parking lot. Their plan is to pick up more charcoal so they can continue grilling the sweet plump corn they've brought from their home in Flagstaff, Arizona.

Miranda and Isaac (Grilled Sweet Corn).

When Tyler and Isaac return, Miranda fills their two large barbecues with the charcoal and then covers the grill with tinfoil clad corn. The show is Isaac's first experience in a Grateful Dead parking lot, and Miranda is thrilled to bring him.

"It's my dog's first show," she explains. "He's doing well. He goes and runs and tries to play with every single dog on the Lot. Even though he's hot, he's happy. Every time you see him, he's got a smile on this face. But tour is hard to do with a dog. You really have to be prepared. I put my dog first. They need attention."

Since 1991 Miranda has been going to see the Dead. She was first introduced to the scene by a friend who liked their music. She has been traveling to shows ever since.

"When I'm inside, there's a certain feeling I get when the Dead start playing and everyone is looking at each other, smiling and hugging. It goes through my whole body and I'm overwhelmed in a good way," says Miranda. "It's an overloading of the senses. You don't need drugs basically, it's all there in front of you. There's family and love and passion and togetherness.

"It's definitely a way of life. It's kind of like an alternative way of living, and that's what really attracted me. You don't have to be stuck in the routine of a nine-to-five job, you can be on the road, making a living and hearing great music. Just meeting really beautiful people twenty-four hours a day. What more could you ask for?

"And it's amazing that this still goes on in 1995. Part of me thinks that somehow, some way, it will keep going. I mean," she says with conviction, "this is in our blood. Just because they stop playing doesn't mean that we'll stop gathering as a family."

Grilled Sweet Corn
Serves 2

"I've sold everything from grilled cheese to bagels with cream cheese and it's just so much work, it doesn't really pay off. Corn is so much simpler and it's in season," says Miranda.

When corn is in season, this is an inexpensive, low-maintenance recipe. It is also an option for vegetarians who like to barbecue. Try barbecuing some seitan (see Glossary) with sauce to match, and have a great dinner.

2 ears of corn
Butter
Lemon pepper
Salt

• Throughout the cooking process, leave the corn in its husk. First, dunk it in water for 2 minutes. Then, wrap in aluminum foil and place on the barbecue. Rotate and let cook for at least 10 minutes. Remember to keep turning as it cooks and watch to see when it's done. Mileage may vary depending on how hot the barbecue gets.
• When you unwrap the tinfoil, the husks should peel off easily.
• Melt on butter, lemon pepper and salt. Try any other spices or herbs on top.

Hidden along a row of cars parked in the grass, Taz, Marshall's Australian shepherd is surrounded by dogs. From time to time, the dogs get their leashes tangled together as they rush around, playing and barking in the shade of Marshall, Sam and Matt's rental car.

Slung from the back of the car, Sam and Matt create their own shade by hanging a tapestry. The shadows keep the sun out and lets them continue sautéing onions for one of their morning selections, Roadside Potatoes.

The plan was to sell food anyway, but when Matt's '84 Volkswagen broke down in Medford, Oregon, on the way to the Portland shows, making money to pay for the rental car became a little more urgent. So the three spent hours preparing spaghetti, pancakes with fresh fruit and Roadside Potatoes.

To get to Portland, Matt, Sam and Marshall traveled from San Francisco through Northern California and Oregon. The traveling, they say, is integral to the Grateful Dead experience.

"Look at Oregon, that's half the trip, coming up here and driving through this incredible place," says Matt. "It's not just the music, it's the whole getting in the car and going. You really feel it when you're driving out of San Francisco and looking at all those people in office

Matt, Sam, Taz and Marshall (Roadside Potatoes). Photo: E. Zipern

26

buildings. But here we are, on our way, see ya!"

"So many people in one place getting so high with the music, just that energy, it's powerful," explains Sam. "A lot of people have preconceptions of the Dead and this whole scene as being just really strange. Strange because it's different. But what is strange? It's just not typical of our society. There's a family feeling at these shows that you don't really experience in society so much."

"Or at any other concert or music for that matter," adds Matt.

"People tend to be a little more together," replies Sam.

"It's definitely a connection in the West Coast," comments Marshall. "And there's the brotherhood which you don't usually find anywhere else. You can, but it's not like this, it's not so free and easy."

Roadside Potatoes
Serves 2

2 Tbs. canola or olive oil

4 large Idaho russet potatoes, cut thin (Matt suggests halving them and then slicing fast. Be careful!)

1/2 red or yellow onion, sliced

Creole seasoning (The seafood seasoning, Old Bay, will work wonderfully too.)

2 to 3 cloves garlic, minced

OPTIONAL

Green and/or red pepper, sliced

Tomato wedges

Fresh basil and/or fresh cilantro, minced

Brown cooked sausage

Monterey Jack and Parmesan cheeses, shredded

Ketchup

Warm tortillas

Salsa

Sour cream

• On a medium flame, heat a pan with just enough oil so that the potatoes don't burn. Once the oil is sizzling, add the potatoes. As they become soft, add onion, Creole seasoning and continue to saute. Ten minutes before done, add the garlic. If you feel like getting crazy, Matt suggests adding green or red peppers, tomato wedges, fresh basil or fresh cilantro or even brown cooked sausage.

• During the last five minutes of cooking, try sprinkling Monterey Jack or Parmesan cheese over the potatoes. Matt says you'll know when it's finished, when A) you can't wait anymore or B) the potatoes are brown and soft.

• Top with ketchup and Creole seasoning, wrap in a warm tortilla and add salsa and sour cream for a breakfast-style burrito.

Elissa Maxwell has been going to see the Grateful Dead for twenty-five years. She first stumbled on the scene by following her brothers.

"I first saw them when I was thirteen years old at Woodstock in Bethel, New York," says Elissa. "My brothers were older than me and they decided that they were going to hitchhike there, and I sort of tagged along. I was very comfortable with the countryside, so it wasn't out of the ordinary, but I was amazed to find out later that they did shut down the roads because of the amount of traffic. There were so many people, but the best part is the way that all different types of people came.

"Shows are like an old family get-together. I might not ever see them for years until they come to Albany. I've had people come up to me and laugh and say, 'I remember you!' I feel like a dinosaur. I look around at so many young faces, I mean, I don't look extremely old, but I'm pushing it.

"For the last ten years, I've made a habit of having my own little costume. Last year I

Elissa (Jammin' Jerry's Jellies). Photo: Mark Dabelstein

came dressed as a chicken. People asked me if I was selling chicken, I said 'No, I'm looking for Little Red Rooster,' and they played that song that night and here I am, strutting around in a chicken outfit!

"Every year I usually have two or three changes of clothes, today I'm just being a wildflower." She explains. "It's just a personality quirk of my own I think. I like imagination, to be different and unique, to wear something that not everyone is wearing. And because it's funny, people laugh at you. They have a good time laughing and I have a good time making them laugh."

To the 1995 shows in Albany, Elissa brought her homemade jams, jellies and biscuits so everyone could taste test her creations.

"The preserves are the best way to get the taste of the fruits at their prime, and not have to worry about spoiling," explains Elissa. "They travel well. Where we live is a very rural area, berry farms and sheep and goats. A good way to spend the day outside is hiking, picking berries. That's what I spend all summer doing."

Elissa makes the preserves at home for herself and her son, Alex Brandon. Besides going berry picking, the two do fun things together in New York State.

"Right now I'm a mother," she says. "I love the chance to relive my childhood and enjoy all these things that I used to love to do, like blow bubbles, and swimming and fishing, and it gives me somebody to share my life with. It gets challenging, they have a little personality of their own. I figured if I got through the first six months, I had it pretty down pat."

Jammin' Jerry's Jellies—Peach Nut Conserve
Makes 7 to 8 1/2 pint jars

"The difference between preserves and conserves is that conserves usually consist of chopped fruit and fruit rinds, nuts and raisins," says Elissa. "Preserves are more the fruit with its own juice.

"The peach nut is something that I concocted on my own. Peaches are very interchangeable with apricots, nectarines, all those fuzzy fruits. If you don't like the lemon, you can use pineapple. I made apricot-pineapple. That was enough to roll over and beg for more." She laughs.

Needed—9 pint-sized jars

1 large seedless orange	1/4 tsp. ground ginger
7 cups peaches, peeled, pitted, and cut into 1/2 inch chunks	1/4 tsp. nutmeg, ground fresh
	1/4 tsp. mace
5 1/2 cups sugar	1/2 cup chopped almonds or pecans
1 can small pineapple chunks	3 Tbs. kirsch or apricot brandy
1/2 tsp. salt	

• With the rind, cut the orange into paper-thin slices. Then, cut each slice into 1/4 inch wedges. (Now they'll be small, thin triangles). Place in a saucepan. Add enough water to cover.
• Cook over low heat until the peel is soft. Place the peaches and oranges in water and the remaining ingredients (except the nuts and kirsch) into a large kettle (pot).
• Boil rapidly and stir frequently until translucent with very little syrup left ("Do not overcook," she says). The conserve will thicken after canning.
• Chopped almonds or pecans and kirsch or apricot brandy may be added 5 minutes before removing the conserve from the heat.
• From the boiling, a layer of foam may rise to the top. Remove the foam, then pour the conserve into hot sterilized jars, 1/8" from the top of the jar. Finish with a boiling water bath for 16 minutes (submerging in hot, boiling water).

"I don't trust just capping them, I always give them the hot water, hot boiling bath afterward," says Elissa. "This way you have a very slim margin to mess them up. Take the little rings, put them upside down and if it doesn't pour out, you know the seal is good."

Elissa recommends the jelly be eaten with homemade buttermilk biscuits, waffles with whipped cream, or as a pancake syrup, although she says the jelly is great to eat by itself. Yum, yum . . .

The day was beautiful. Sunny, bright, clean sweet air hung above the bright, green fields outside of Indianapolis. Scheduled at the Deer Creek Music Center, to get there one simply had to make his or her way around fields and farms and trees and down rolling roads. Though as night fell, an eerie feeling began to settle into the air.

The show was about to end as Marc and Erica sat in the shell of their truck, preparing to sell water and Tamari Roasted Hemp Seeds to masses of thirsty and hungry Deadheads. Moist night air descended firmly upon the grassy hill next to the venue, some distance from the separate Shakedown parking lot where Marc and Erica were parked.

On the hill, madness had broken out. People leaving the show passed police officers suited in riot gear. Dogs alert and at attention and vibes of panic filled the air. What the fans could not have possibly missed were the over one thousand people breaking down the fence during the Dead's first set to rush inside.

But the mayhem was not as obvious to those in the parking lots. Marc and Erica talk about the Grateful Dead and remember the good. The beautiful things about going to a Dead show. As they talk, they wish they were inside. In moments like these, when troubles surrounding Dead shows seem overwhelming, it is good to recount the positive, the first Grateful Dead experiences which attracted us.

"My first show was Hartford, 1990 spring tour," begins Marc. "It was awesome, one of the best experiences of my life. I'm a singer. When I was in high school, I was always into music but I never really experienced rock concerts before because I was young. Though my family was very musical, I was never able to go see concerts. A friend of mine took me. For being my first concert, I could not have asked for any other band. I fell in love by the end of the show. Also, it was the first time I did LSD, the first time I ever really experienced something different than drinking and smoking pot, and it opened my eyes to so many things. I never saw so much color in my life, it was great, and at that time a lot more people wore tie-dyes so it was a whole new experience of so much color. And the show . . . I sat in my seat . . . it was so funny, I went to the seat that I was supposed to sit in and it was up in the bleachers, in the upper deck. It was incredible, and from there on, I was hooked.

"It was the first time I ever experienced all these people coming together and celebrating something. Maybe it was celebrating the Grateful Dead, but it was also celebrating this freedom, this free spirit type of lifestyle where people could come together with food, good food and hugs and smiles and that was really new. Coming from a small town, I didn't see it. Both men and women with long hair, just people looking different. And along with the community of people, was the musical aspect of the show. It was nice for me because I could do what I wanted to do. I could be myself and didn't feel I had to act a certain way, or dance a certain way because there were all different types of people and wherever you went, everybody was different, no matter where you looked. The spinners were over here, and they were all into their thing and the tapers were there, and they were into their thing, and the Phil Zone was there and they were into their thing. And I was here into my own thing. Everybody had their own thing, and it was awesome. It was very diverse in that way, and the music was just incredible. I remember being high and floating on the notes through the arena.

"I felt I was actually bouncing off notes on these big staffs going across the stadium. Huge staffs with colorful notes. I would see the notes on the staff going up and down the way the notes were being played. It was just amazing to me. But, times have changed, I listen more, rather than see more, I have a different focus now than before. Just by listening to the music, I get high. Sometimes I'll just stand there for a long time and I'll listen but I won't dance. I wish I was in the show." He smiles thinking about it.

"My first show was spring tour of '92, Hampton, Virginia, which is a really nice place to see a first show," explains Erica. "There are fountains and really nice tree walkway areas. It was just really magical for me, it was a totally different reality than I had been in before. When I first went it definitely opened me up to that there was something else. There was something else that was different from my reality that I could experience.

"If I am in touch with the music I feel like I really get a strong message or a strong sense of direction. It has happened to me less this tour, there was a time that I was really in touch with the music, and I was going through a lot of stuff about trying to work on myself and trying to be open. And I really felt a strong message from the music about letting go and trying to work things out and be open to what was going on. The music has been an amazing force in my life, the lyrics and the dance. I definitely feel like dancing helps me connect with the music a lot more."

"I see it in her," Marc says, smiling. "It's amazing. The first show that we went to together was Shoreline in '94, last September, and we were hanging out in the pit on Jerry's side. I've known Erica for a long time, but it was the first time that I actually saw this amazing excitement. She's an exciting person, but she doesn't show this excitement in everyday life. It was great to see. I was watching her and she was dancing and her smile was big. It was amazing, awesome. Finally, I see where the passion just comes right in . . . and it's . . . the Grateful Dead."

"I don't necessarily believe in divinity outside of myself. I believe that every person has this inner divinity and all that religion is, is allowing people to really connect with the inner God or Goddess that's inside of them, not in the ego sense at all, but just in the pure being. I feel like dancing and the music really helps me align to that. To reach that high potential in the present moment, that's clear.

"That's definitely different for me, too, because that inner God, or that inner divinity, I used to believe in something exterior. I definitely believe that it's all general forces that are working together. That's like Jerry's divinity too. I think he is in his highest sense of self when he is playing."

"Definitely, I think so," adds Marc. "I mean, they wouldn't be doing it for thirty years. This is like pure joy for them. I don't think they're doing it because they think they have a job to do. Especially this tour, they've really been rocking, and it's unfortunate that I haven't been grounded enough to enjoy it as much as I used to. I just think there's a lot of other things that I'm really focused on right now, and that's hard for me."

"The Grateful Dead are one of the best things that's ever happened to me," says Erica.

"Me too," adds Marc. "A catalyst for where I am right now. I think that the Grateful Dead was the first step toward where I am right now. I think they've definitely helped me grow to

Tamari Roasted Hemp Seeds
*Makes 2 cups of hemp seeds to eat,
cook with and share with friends*

"One of the reasons that we got into it is we wanted to do something that was really healthy. We were trying to think of an idea to sell something extra that would open people's eyes and get people going," says Marc. "It's a good service. It's not beer, it's not drugs and it's totally healthy for you and everybody needs it.

"People were laughing at it saying, 'Can we grow them?'" he continues. "I'm like 'No, this is protein, this is good for you, this is the best thing on the Lot you will find, it's the most healthy. Have water and hemp seeds and you'll be fine for the day if you have no money and nothing to eat.'"

"I've always wanted to provide good healthy food," explains Erica. "I think that people don't know about them, there's not enough consciousness about hemp products. There's so much emphasis on the psychoactive part of it. There is an emphasis on getting high and that's sad, but I definitely think that it's more than just here. It's everywhere. There is such a prejudice against hemp.

"I feel like I did open some people's eyes up and people tried them that wouldn't have tried them and I talked to people about how good they are for you. We definitely did some educating," she says. "I educated myself, because I didn't know that much about the hemp industry at all. I knew before that it was awesome but I didn't know how good the seeds were for you, how good the fiber is and all the products you can make from this incredible plant."

"It is an incredible plant. It's a wonder plant. I think it's the plant that's going to save the earth," proclaims Marc. "I mean if anything is going to save the earth, hemp is going to do it."

2 cups hemp seeds
2 to 4 Tbs. tamari, or to taste

• Cleaning them first is an important process. To clean the seeds, put water into a pitcher, add the seeds and stir. Gently pour the seeds out into a colander. When you pour them off, all the pebbles, rocks and dirt will sink to the bottom. Then, rinse again while in the colander.
• While they're still wet, pour the hemp seeds into a hot frying pan, wok or cast iron skillet and continually stir them on high (they burn very easily). Constantly stir for 5 to 10 minutes until crunchy. When they're done they'll start to pop and have a nutty smell. Taste and smell them so you know if they are starting to burn.
• As soon as they start to pop, turn the heat down and pour the tamari (use lots if you like them salty) and mix so all the seeds are coated. Keep stirring until the seeds become dry. Also, try roasting the seeds with spices and herbs. Try cayenne, dill and black pepper.
• Marc and Erica say the seeds taste best cold, so let them sit or place in the fridge to cool. After they cool, store in a Ziplock bag in the fridge, freezer or anything airtight.

where I am," he continues. "They were the beginning to me, they opened me up to what is out there. I was lucky enough to see beyond it or blessed enough to see that the Grateful Dead isn't the end, the Grateful Dead is not the answer. It's part of the answer. For me it's the first step to get there—it's the openness, it's the communication, it's the community, it's the love, it's the music, it's the dancing, it's living your life, it's being a free spirit and enjoying your life, and that's it."

"I had this dream, there was this platform in the middle of the ocean, and it was sort of high up and there was a ladder coming down from it, and somehow I got to the platform and this modern glass building was on top of it," explains Erica. "I went in and Jerry was there and he played. He went into the studio and wanted to play this new song for me, so he played this new song and then he and I went into this green room. It was a room with green couches and green carpeting and we just talked for a long time. I don't really remember what we talked about, but it was this in-depth conversation. And then I said, 'I'm ready to leave now, I want to go,' and he walked me down this corridor and we walked to the edge of the platform and he gave me a hug, and I said good-bye. He was the same size as I was, except he was a little bit pudgier, and he said, 'If you ever need anything you know where to come.' I left and I went down the ladder, and that was the breaking point from when I really needed the Grateful Dead for their whole essence, or survival and spirituality. Now when I go back I can use the Grateful Dead as a reference point to where I am in my life."

More Decadent and Delectable Main Dishes

❀ ♥ ❀

Tofu Pot Pie
Makes 1 pie

"I added oregano to the dough for flavor," says Chase. "I also added a few things to the gravy. I like a lot of spices. We also used potatoes instead of tofu, just because it's easier to keep potatoes on the road."

THE CRUST
1 cup flour
1 Tb. baking powder
1/4 cup oil
1 1/2 Tbs. water
2 Tbs. oregano
Salt to taste

VEGETABLE FILLING
2 cups potatoes or tofu, cut in
  1/2 inch cubes
2 carrots, diced
1/2 cup corn

1/2 cup peas
1/2 cup onions, chopped
2 cloves garlic, minced

GRAVY
1 cup flour
1/3 cup nutritional yeast
2 Tbs. soy sauce
2 Tbs. oil
1/2 cup water
Garlic powder to taste
Salt and pepper to taste

- To begin, mix the crust ingredients into a soft dough. When soft, roll it out into a thin layer and add flour as you roll to keep it from sticking. Next, cover the bottom of a pie pan with the dough. Save some dough for the end to cover the pie.
- Boil or steam the potatoes and carrots, drain and place in a skillet. Add corn, peas, onions and garlic and heat.
- Over a low flame, combine the gravy ingredients in another skillet and add water until a watery consistency is obtained. Take off the heat when thick and bubbly. Mix with the vegetables.
- Pour the vegetable-gravy filling into the bottom of the pie pan and cover with another thin piece of dough. Close the edges under the rim of the pie pan.
- Bake at 350° for 20 to 30 minutes or until the crust is golden brown.

*See Rich's Vegan Burritos in the "Food to Roll With" chapter.

The faded blue carpet on the hotel room floor is randomly covered with withered pieces of carrot, lettuce and tiny smatterings of rice and pinto beans. The savory bits narrowly missed being stuffed into large flour tortillas to then be covered with homemade salsa. In every space throughout the small, crowded room are knives, cutting boards and a surplus of leftover vegetables.

Although the proprietors of this particular Econo Lodge in Charlotte, North Carolina, probably wouldn't give their blessings to such activity, Chase and Rich have spent hours before each of the 1995 Dead shows at the Charlotte Coliseum preparing to vend their enormous, stuffed, vegan burritos.

When they can, Chase and Rich try to sell one of their legendary vegan creations. Usually, it is Tofu Pot Pie with fresh salad on the side, vegan burritos or banana and carrot breads.

They began vending during the summer tour of 1993. Since then, they've traveled to almost every show in their dark green school bus, along the way rolling hundreds of vegetable stuffed burritos and filling their oven full of crisp, baked Tofu Pot Pies.

To help refine the Tofu Pot Pie recipe, Chase and Rich invited other food vendors on the Lot to taste test the pies and offer suggestions.

"We had all of our friends and the vendors try it and give us their opinions," says Chase. "That helped. They liked it. A friend of ours that sells pizza gave us a few pointers."

"We gave them to the Egg Roll People and the Burrito People, and everyone just keeps coming back," adds Rich. "It's like the newest thing on the Lot. We wanted to get out of burritos because we make these really killer burritos and they're kind of high-maintenance. So we're trying something low-maintenance, but this doesn't seem to be much lower maintenance, just more fun, and it's a new thing."

On days when shows are scheduled, Chase and Rich get to the Lot early in the morning to find a good vending spot on the Shakedown. There they vend and then clean up late into the night, a system which allows them very little sleep.

"Since we started doing all this, we normally sleep about four or five hours a night, and then get up and start doing things," says Chase. "Five hours is a good night."

"Three hours is a normal night," adds Rich.

"But we do take care of ourselves," Chase continues. "I mean we eat well, and if we're tired, we'll sleep in. To me, it's not worth getting sick over."

Supporting themselves by vending food allows them to go into as many shows as they can. Sometimes, they take a break and opt to sit out for a night or two.

"We went into all the shows on the West Coast, so I'm like, 'Okay, I can sit out for a few, because that doesn't happen all that much,'" explains Chase. "The last couple tours, we went without any tickets and we went into most of the shows, making money selling food and then we'd buy tickets. Every once in a while, I get in this mood where I'd love to go in, but I'm not wholeheartedly into it, so I just sit out and it makes me appreciate it more when I do go inside. I've passed tickets up before, just because I know other people would appreciate it more than I would at that point. Every once in a while it's good for me to sit out and then the next time I go inside, then it's that much more exciting for me."

Chase and Rich (Tofu Pot Pie and Rich's Vegan Burritos). Photo: E. Zipern

Emanating from the dirt parking lot across from the Birmingham-Jefferson Civic Center, aromas from Allison Wonderland's fragrant Indian dish can be detected from great distances. The lush, creamy, tomato-red curry cuddling eight different vegetables and a smorgasbord of spices creates an extraordinarily aromatic and esthetically pleasing smell.

When Allison, her new dog, Snagglepuss, and their friend Cheryl ventured east from San Francisco for the Dead's spring tour, they decided to cook Coco Veggie Curry, hoping to provide a delectable dish that everyone in the Lot would relish. With the rich scent of coconut milk, tomatoes and spices simmering, Deadheads throughout the Lot invariably seemed to end up at their parking spot.

Allison and Cheryl (Coco Veggie Curry).
Photo: E. Zipern

"This is a great dish to feed meat eaters who don't eat anything green," Allison says, smiling. "People who hate vegetarian food usually love this. It's really fun to turn them onto some food when all they think is, 'Who wants to eat vegetarian food? It's just a bunch of sprouts, or yogurt of something.'"

As she cooks, Allison pauses to look over at her altar; a small table standing to the side of her car. It holds rocks, pink and purple flowers, shells, jewelry and a big, thick, beautiful head of garlic. The altar and its offerings remind her of the earth, so she always takes it on her travels.

"It keeps me connected with what is important," Allison explains. "Like sometimes I get stressed out. Food spills, I'm not making money, whatever. I go 'Ahhhhh!' If I can just look at the altar, I'm back where I'm supposed to be. I collect things along the road. These little flowers," she says, pointing to the tiny purple blossoms sitting in a jar on the table. "They kinda pay homage to the space I'm using and give thanks for the food I'm able to cook, appreciate the joy of life . . . and I love the garlic on there. I like to put some of the food that I'm using to cook with there."

As they cook, Allison and Cheryl talk to Snagglepuss. Snagglepuss is a small, cream-colored, odd-toothed Pekinese-terrier mix who attempts to look fierce by growling slightly and kicking up dust as various Lot dogs, much larger than he, walk by. "Hey . . . Snagglepuss, you mellow out!" Allison shouts to the dog as he snarls. "He's a dork, isn't he?" She laughs.

Allison began listening to the Grateful Dead when she was five and went to her first show with her sister at twelve. Allison estimates she has seen around four hundred shows.

The Grateful Dead played a large part in her adolescence.

"When I went to my first Dead show, I saw all these people with license plates from different states. I thought, 'Wow, how cool, a big traveling circus.' I've always wanted to run away and join the circus, so I did.

"I love the words to their songs, even though they forget 'em most of the time," she says. "I mean, my sister used to sing me 'Ripple' when I was a child and I thought she wrote it. When I first heard it playing at somebody's house on a record, I was like, 'Hey, this is my sister's song.' So I kinda grew up on the music.

"I think that as much as the music, it is this possibility. There's a lot of sharing that I don't see in most other places. There's a lot of beautiful people, a lot of inspiring people. And a lot of confused, lost people that need to meet the beautiful inspiring people. I've been both while I've been here. I think I go back and forth still. I have days of being lost, and days of being inspiring."

In 1991 Allison took a break from the Grateful Dead. Camping in the Lot had recently been abolished and vending restrictions were being enforced more than ever, so much so that she found herself getting thrown in jail for vending T-shirts. Allison decided to stop touring for a while. During that time, she toured with a rock band as their cook, lived in Hawaii, Arizona, and basically traveled the world. Now, back on the Lot, she is able to reflect on how the scene has changed.

"The scene is a lot less cohesive than it used to be," she reasons. "Back in the days when you could camp in these kinds of Lots, the vegetarian, vegan, kinda macrobiotic people had to camp next to the people that ate meat and they had to camp next to the people that drank a lot of alcohol and they had to camp next to the dread kids and they had to camp next to the girls who wore makeup and everyone was a lot closer together. Now that the hotel scene is happening, the campgrounds are more separated. I think that has caused a lot of problems in the scene. I think that causes the cliquishness which we're all trying to get away from.

"The police are a much more intense influence these days. They used to kinda just make sure people didn't get hurt. Now, they seem to make sure they hurt people. The police, their influence is scary. People can't be more creative with what they do with the scene. I think that it's still the same kind of spiritual experience for people if they can get over that step. It's like the police try to start riots and security, they want you to get mad and agro the way they are. I've done that a few times, and I've found that if you can just stay beautiful throughout the whole thing, then the scene will stay strong and they really can't rip it apart. But they're button pushers, you know?"

Allison has always cooked at Dead shows. A few years back she worked with her friend's stir-fry company, "Not Fuck Around Productions." During the Dead's 1995 summer tour, Allison and Cheryl plan to cook various summer tour specialities such as, fresh fruit tarts, scones for breakfast and sticky buns—all foods she was unable to eat when she was trying to stay macrobiotic (see Glossary), on the road.

Coco Veggie Curry
Serves 4 to 6

This is Allison's rendition of an Indian dish, and it is really good! Allison doesn't follow an exact recipe, so it turns out differently every time.

2 Tbs. canola oil
1/2 tsp. mustard seeds
3 to 5 cloves fresh garlic (use as much as you feel like mincing)
1 fresh jalapeno pepper, sliced
1 onion, cut in chunks
2 big chopped tomatoes or 1 28 oz. can whole, crushed, sauce or stewed tomatoes (you can use more if needed)
1 cinnamon stick
1 can unsweetened coconut milk
At least 1 to 2 fat tsps. curry. Allison sometimes uses up to 1/4 a cup!

Soy sauce or sea salt (to bring out the flavor of the curry)
1 sweet potato, sliced 1/4 inch thick
1 regular variety potato, sliced 1/4 inch thick
1/2 pound of carrots, sliced in big chunks
1/4 head broccoli and/or 1/4 head cauliflower, cut in florets
1 green pepper, sliced
1/4 cup sliced shiitake mushrooms
1 cup brown basmati or jasmine rice
A few whole small mushrooms (regular variety)
A couple of whole cherry tomatoes
Cashews and peanuts

* "Use any vegetables," says Allison. "Don't be picky."

• Heat 2 tablespoons of canola oil in a large saute pan. Add the mustard seeds and continue to heat until they pop. This will take less than a minute, depending on the pan and the degree of heat you use. As soon as they begin to pop, remove the pan from the heat so the seeds don't burn. If they burn, start over again. Allison says it will ruin the flavor. "With mustard seeds or garlic, if either of them burn, you should always start over again, with any recipe," she says.
• Now add the garlic, using as much as you feel like chopping. Cut a fresh jalapeno pepper. "Don't bother using it if it's not fresh," she says. "Put in something else instead." Throw it into the wok. Add the onion and continue to cook. Stir on a low heat until the onions are translucent. Then, add a bunch of fresh tomatoes, chopped, or a big can of tomatoes. Just add enough to make a red curry.
• Add 1 whole cinnamon stick. "I put extra cinnamon in all my food," Allison says. "I think it's more delicious that way. I like a lot of cinnamon in my curry. You should always have a few cinnamon sticks in your kitchen. I also like to use a lot of Indian spices whole."

→

- Now add the coconut milk. This, Allison says, turns it into a "kinda milky globular mixture of coconut and tomato." Add curry to taste. "I'd start with a good, fat tablespoon or two, and it might go anywhere up to a quarter of a cup depending on how strong the curry is," she says. "There is a lot of different kinds of curry. I use 1/4 cup in mine because I like it spicy. People who aren't used to curry should probably start with less. If you use spicy curry, you have to be careful, because it can get bitter if you use too much."
- Add water to thin if needed. Sprinkle a little soy sauce but if you don't have any, use sea salt. It brings out the flavor of the curry. Add the sweet and regular potatoes. Cover and let cook for about 10 to 15 minutes or until the potatoes are slightly soft.
- Now, add the vegetables. The veggies should soften just a little. First add the carrots, then the broccoli and cauliflower for they are the hardest vegetables. Let that cook, then add the green pepper and then the shiitake mushrooms.
- Make the rice while the coco-curry continues to cook, but make sure the veggies stay crisp. During the last 5 minutes of cooking, add the whole mushrooms and tomatoes.
- Serve over rice and top with chopped cashews and peanuts. Enjoy this, it's a good one!

"I used to be macro-neurotic and I'm over it." She laughs. "I travel around the world and I like to eat with people that aren't the same as me. I don't always like to exclude myself from everyone just to nourish my body. I think your mind and spirit has power over what you put in your body. Not that what you put in your body isn't important, that's why I'm making vegan curry veggies for everyone, but if you get too caught up in it, it just really dominates your life. It's all you can think about. Especially if you're traveling on the road, and you're macrobiotic and you're living in a car, and you have to eat six meals a day. You're like, trying to make seaweed in microwave ovens across America in truck stops. Once in a while, it's not so bad to sit down and eat a white flour biscuit with some jam.

"But it's nice to turn people on to this kind of food, because if you won't eat with them, they won't eat with you. That's the way it is. I cook a lot of times in San Francisco. Two of my really good friends are homeless there. I love it because they bring a couple of their friends over and I bring some of my friends. And we sit down on the floor of my apartment and just eat and laugh and share and connect. I think that's the problem with America. That's where the family is screwed. It's not that there's no family. It's just that people don't celebrate life together enough. You know, the primal experience is mostly gone. That's another thing about the Dead. Look around. People are playing drums, they're eating hallucinogenic plants, they're eating food together, they're washing babies together, they're coming together to create a positive vibration."

The square white vinyl tent, heavy with puddles of freshly fallen rain, shelters Mongo, his stir-fry partner, Jeff, and their Wokin' Blues table from the continual downpours around the RFK Stadium parking lots. The soggy area is a daily gathering spot for numerous groups in the Grateful Dead scene.

Before the day begins, vendor friends commune under the tent as Mongo and Jeff dedicate hours to preparing stir-fry. As show time draws near, the covering becomes an impromptu assemblage of the taper section and an occasional meeting place for other Wharf Rat friends.

"There's a lot of closeness here between people," explains Mongo. "I feed all my taper friends, I feed all my family, people that I live with in Northern California, that I travel with and the vendors. We all pull for each other. When somebody runs out of something we're always there for each other, and the same with the Wharf Rats. These guys all know where I am most of them will come by during the course of the day."

Mongo and Jeff (Wokin' Blues Stir-Fry).
Photo: Mark Dabelstein

Like other vendors, Mongo and Jeff lead a hectic life while on tour. Nights before shows are spent chopping onions, carrots, broccoli and squash, while the mornings have them rushing to the Lot early to get a good position on the Shakedown. With prepping and then selling, cleaning up and breaking down, Mongo and Jeff usually spend at least fifteen hours per show day in the parking lot.

And if he isn't working with stir-fry, Mongo is taping the show. A longtime taper, Mongo never misses a show or the opportunity to copy a show he doesn't have in his collection of close to one thousand tapes.

"Originally I felt that if I was going to be here, I should be more involved with something other than running around in the parking lot before the show," Mongo explains. "I traded tapes for the first two years and then a friend of mine talked me into buying a tape deck. I taped my first show and I was hooked. There's a certain thing about being able to go in there and then walking out with the best possible copy of the show that these guys are giving away. Jerry said it a bunch of times, 'Once I've played it, it's yours to have.'

"You go to some venues and the sound is horrible and the taper section is way in the back of the stadium. RFK and Giants stadiums are horrible, but we're tapers, that's what we do. If I'm going to a show, I'm going to run my equipment in there and run my tape decks. You never

41

know when it was some-body's first show or whatever the occasion might be."

The 1995 summer tour marked the twenty-first anniversary since Mongo's first show and his fourth year of staying clean. In the last several years, Mongo has made the decision to stay on tour, as he feels part of the Grateful Dead family.

"I went and saw Merle Saunders one night and I had only been clean for about eight months. I heard Merle do, 'I want to thank you for letting me be myself again.' And this whole spiritual thing just happened right there. After that date, I saw

Wokin' Blues Stir-Fry
Serves 4

1 Tb. sesame oil
1 cup each green and red cabbage
1 cup carrots (2 to 3 carrots when sliced)
1 onion
1 stalk celery
1 yellow squash
1 green squash

1 bunch broccoli
1 Tb. fresh garlic, minced
1 Tb. fresh ginger, minced
1 tsp. white pepper, to taste
Soy sauce, to taste
1/4 orange or 1 tablespoon fresh-squeezed orange juice
Cooked rice (any kind)

*All vegetables are cut julienne

• Heat the wok and add the sesame oil. (Remember, hot wok, cold oil!) Throw the vegetables in, toss until coated and add the seasonings.
• Continue to saute and when the onions turn opaque, sprinkle on soy sauce. Add the juice of a fresh orange (or fresh-squeezed orange juice) at the end. Serve over rice.

fifty-three Grateful Dead concerts in a row, and in the midst of doing that I realized I didn't have a job, and if I wanted to be here I had to support myself, so I started selling stir-fry. Since then I decided that I don't want to stop touring. I don't want to miss shows, I don't want to miss when the boys break out with something, I would hate myself.

"This past year I took the fall tour off, I moved into a place in California, I got myself a job and I hated it. I missed being with my friends, I missed being with my family and that was really rough. I spent like forty-five dollars just calling the Dead lines to find out what they played and I was miserable the whole time.

"It's definitely spiritual for me, but then vending and taping have lost some of that origi-nal spirituality. The pressure of taping and vending sometimes takes its toll on the show. But that's the percentage thing, if I'm going to be at every show this year, I'm bound to have a few bad ones and I've accepted that, and I've learned to go in there with a clear conscience and not look for my favorites but look for what's going on."

Vegan Taco Salad
Makes 4 salads or a nice casserole

This is an incredibly delicious dish. If made into a casserole, it becomes a warm bean, vegetable and spice meal. If on a salad, it's just as wonderful.

2 Tbs. vegetable oil
1 white onion, chopped
4 to 5 large cloves garlic, minced (more to taste as always)
1 small to medium zucchini, cut in circles, then moons
1 yellow squash, cut in circles, then moons
Cayenne to taste
4 tsps. cumin (or more, they like to use a lot)

3 cups cooked or canned beans (Use whatever you have around. Some good ones to use are black beans, dark kidney beans and pinto beans)
1 cup corn
Cilantro, to taste
Salsa
Corn tortillas
Lettuce
Cheese or Soy cheese, optional

• To prepare the vegetable-bean mixture, saute the onions and garlic in oil, then add the zucchini, yellow squash, cayenne and cumin and cook until soft. Next add the beans, corn and cilantro and saute.
• To make a casserole, layer the ingredients in a casserole dish. Layer the salsa on the bottom, then corn tortillas, and then vegetable-bean mixture. Continue layering in order. Adding cheese or soy cheese is always optional. Bake at around 300° for about 25 minutes. (Just long enough for the flavors to meld and the cheese to melt—if you eat diary.)
• To just make a taco salad (instead of a casserole), simply lay the sauteed vegetable-bean mixture over lettuce and corn chips and top with salsa.

Their house is a '66 light blue Chevy school bus that gets seven miles to the gallon. When they're not taking their home on tour or traveling to Rainbow Gatherings, Donyele and Nat park their house in Colorado and North Carolina. For three years, the vehicle has been home.

Dark redwood floors, the smell of cooking food and the aroma of cedar chips from their dogs' beds gives the bus a dank, warm, homey feel. The vehicle sports a bed, table, storage space and blue flowered curtains covering the windows. In the kitchen, everything has its place, as a plethora of spices, tinctures and baking ingredients cover the shelves.

Built by a carpenter, the long bus is constructed of scrap wood and other essentials to keep warm in the cold Colorado winters. The walls, floor and ceiling are insulated, a wood-burning stove sits across from the aqua-colored double oven and solar panels perched atop the roof provide electricity.

"I like having a home that I can move around. I like the lifestyle," explains Nat.

"Eventually I think we might have enough money to get land or be in a situation that might change, but for right now, I'm enjoying it. I like being on the road, I like the Grateful Dead."

On their way back to live in Colorado, carrying everything they owned, Donyele and Nat stopped at the RFK shows before hitting the Rainbow Gathering in New Mexico. To pay for the stops they sold vegan taco salad, an easier dish than the pizza they vended on the previous summer tour. Donyele and Nat love going to the shows, but both get tired of vending.

"If I could afford to just come to the show, and go into the show and not have to work, that's what I would do," says Donyele. "The music gets me high."

Nat and Donyele's three dogs accompany them wherever they go. The three were born in the car and have since spent their lives on the road. Nat's dog, Althea, gave birth to the puppies as the couple was leaving a 1989 Rainbow Gathering in Nevada. The two ended up raising the litter after Althea bolted the day after giving birth.

"We've had these dogs since the day they were born," Donyele explains. "The day after they were born, their mom jumped out of the car after we had just left the Rainbow Gathering in Nevada. I don't know what happened. We were driving down the highway at fifty-five miles an hour and she jumped out of the car. We looked for her for hours and hours—no sign of her whatsoever. So we bottle-fed the litter, there were nine puppies. A friend of ours took two, so we bottle-fed seven puppies and kept three of them. We were on tour, and it was the only time we ever spare changed. We were spare changing for puppy food because the formula we had to make was canned milk, honey or maple syrup, molasses, eggs and water. It was really expensive."

Donyele and Nat named the dogs—Bela (after the old horror film actor Bela Lugosi), Mountain Dog and Althea. Now almost six, the three go everywhere their people do, including Dead shows (except for Las Vegas shows where Donyele says it's too hot for them.) The dogs sleep in the bus on their cedar beds, or sometimes they take over their owners' bed.

"Traveling with them is fine," says Donyele. "They keep me company, I love to be with them. I hate when I have to leave them behind anywhere. I see a lot of people who don't give their dogs enough water, truck them around all day. But I think it's easier for us because we live in our school bus. Their dog food is always there, their water is always there. They're home."

Nat, Donyele and Friends (Vegan Taco Salad).
Photo: E. Zipern

It is an unusually warm spring afternoon in Memphis, Tennessee, and Jeff Cahill has been standing out in the hot sun all day. Because of the heat, everything black is extremely hot, including the pavement, the cars and the two twelve-gallon dark black pots that sit in front of him. Since late morning, Jeff has stood behind the large pots, stirring, spicing and preparing Mississippi Uptown Jambalaya, a delicious Southern specialty.

"Ya can't beat it . . . best food in Memphis!" he yells out frequently, enticing others to adventure in the delicious spiciness of the dish. Because of the overwhelming number of food vendors in the Lot, Jeff worries that his dish won't sell.

"I'd like to feed some more people," he laments, "but people are a little sketchy because I'm not family. I've only been to about fourteen shows, and this is my first time vending. We worked hard to make some good food, so hopefully people will start eating it. But it's cool. Right when we got here this morning, this dude, Spaghetti Freddy, came over and started helping us out. He said he had been touring since '76. We told him that we had some kick-ass jambalaya and right away, he helped us set up and gave us a couple pointers. That was pretty cool."

Jeff's vending troubles probably have more to do with the particulars associated with serving a nonvegetarian version of jambalaya to a group whose vegetarian members reign. Plenty of carnivores did eventually find him and by the end of the night, he was sold out. But the kick behind jambalaya, the reason it tastes so good—meat or no meat—is in the blend of spices.

"It's just one of those Creole dishes that combines all kinds of spices, and it comes up with maximum flavor," he explains. Jeff learned to make the dish from an old friend he worked with.

"I worked at a micro brewery in North Hampton, Massachusetts. One of the dudes I worked with was getting way into Cajun cooking, so we took a lot of adventures and tried out a lot of stuff."

Jeff went to his first show in '91 when a girlfriend brought him. "I had never been to a show," he remembers. "When she introduced me to it, none of my friends were Deadheads, and I kinda just brought everybody. I said, 'You guys gotta check this out!' I've introduced upward of probably twelve peo-

Jeff (Mississippi Uptown Jambalaya).
Photo: E. Zipern

45

ple, all of whom love it now. This is the only place I can think of where you can go and hang out with eighty thousand people, who are all as chill as you are. Especially because it breaks up the reality a little bit."

Jeff brought his friend Marty to the Memphis show. Marty had never gone before, and when tickets were scarce, Jeff gave him his own ticket.

"I haven't been to a show since August '94, and Marty had never gone, so I let him get a ticket and go into the show, and I stayed behind," says Jeff. "He loved it. It's an instant addiction. He was born and raised in Mississippi and never got into it. Now he wants to go and do this for a whole summer. I think he might. I mean, I got my job back in Massachusetts for the summer, but I think I might have to forego it!"

Mississippi Uptown Jambalaya
Serves 6 to 10

1/2 cup olive oil
1 med. onion, diced or roughly chopped
2 cloves (or more) fresh garlic, minced
2 stalks celery, coarsely chopped
 *Spices—paprika (use lots), oregano, cayenne, sage, chili powder, Creole seasoning (use lots), dry mustard, thyme, lots of hot sauce (Tabasco). 1 tsp. each of white and black pepper. Use a big pinch of each. All spices really are to taste, so don't be afraid!
 *Vegetables—Jeff suggests using any combination of the following vegetables in any amount, so use your imagination! (Though don't feel limited by these veggies.)
Okra
Corn
Yellow squash or zucchini
Eggplant
1 bell pepper, diced
Sherry to taste
2 15 oz. cans whole, crushed or stewed tomatoes
1 cup each pinto and kidney beans, cooked soft or canned
1/2 cup lentils or bulgur, uncooked
3 cups rice

• In olive oil, saute the onion, garlic, celery and the spices. Then, add the other vegetables and throw in some sherry. Add the stewed tomatoes, the beans and the lentils or bulgur.
• Cook the rice in the water you used to cook the beans (if you used dry beans) and add that into the mixture last, along with more water if needed.
• Season to taste and let simmer for at least 45 minutes to 1 hour, but simmer as long as possible. Jambalaya should come out spicy, thick and hearty.

The dusty, gravel filled, chaotic parking lot near The Omni in Atlanta is jam packed with vendors, dogs, vehicles and a mass of people checking out the Shakedown. To accommodate the overflow, another Shakedown materializes across the street in a parking lot lined with billowy, purple flowered Mimosa trees.

Jeff Jones and friends anchored themselves on a fuzzy blue blanket beneath the bright hazy sky. Resting on Jeff's new green Coleman stove are two shiny silver stainless steel pots filled with thick, savory Red Beans and Rice, simmering and speckled with basil, oregano and chili peppers.

"I'm addicted to red beans, rice and pasta," Jeff explains. "I practically live off the stuff. Beans and rice are easy to fix, really filling and not too complicated. I generally use all organic ingredients if I can find them, but in the South for some reason, it's really hard. Out in California it seems like natural food stores are in every itty-bitty town. Here it's not the same at all.

"It seems like so many people aren't aware of the value of what they eat these days," he asserts. "That's one of the greatest things about cooking on the Lot. People do appreciate when you're really conscious about what you cook. Too many people spend their money on hot dogs and Wendy's and this and that. The energy from organic food is so much different, so much better, not just for your body, but for your mind and soul as well. If I can turn a few people onto that, I mean, I've done my job. Food for body and thought, I guess."

Clad in a multicolored tie-dye and jeans with the occasional hole, Jeff smiles when he speaks. He truly is happy where he's at, providing good food for people and being a part of the Lot scene.

Jeff (Red Beans and Rice). Photo: E. Zipern

"This is my fifth year on tour," he comments. "Provided I get in tonight and tomorrow night, tomorrow will be my fiftieth show. It's kinda funny that every year that I'm in Atlanta, I'm completely burnt. I do better two thousand miles away from home then I do in my hometown," he adds, "It's kind of a hard Lot here, and a lot of times, a hard ticket."

Though he has traveled all over the country to see the Dead, Jeff went to the Atlanta shows, thirty miles from where he grew up, for one last time before he leaves the region.

"I'm looking to leave," he explains. "I've lived in so many different places, but I always seem to end up back here. I'll keep doing tour for as long as I can and as long as I'm living somewhere I agree with, hopefully in the Rocky Mountains. Just work a job, do tour, work a job, do tour, that same old pattern." He laughs.

"My first show was in Atlanta in 1990 and it did me right," Jeff explains. "Even before that I was listening to the albums. And then I went to a Dead show, and I'm just like, 'Geez, I had no idea this sort of thing existed.' I had no point of reference to really understand what was going on. I've always been a freak. But I never knew what really went on at a Dead show. I dug it totally. I dropped out of college and ran around, and it's been going on for five years.

"It is a lot more than the music," he continues. "It's our own world that you can slip in and out of. To me, it's the whole thing that Deadheads are involved with outside of tour, whether it's going to Gatherings or just going and staying in a national park or someplace. It seems like it's a lot of people who don't really get what this whole society is about and are trying to rid themselves of all the bullshit that makes life difficult, even as far as paying rent. Just get it out of your life, 'cause things are so much happier. When you don't have all those worries that come with living a straight life, it just unfolds, your life unfolds in a totally amazing way. I don't think there's any amount of money that can replace the experiences that I've had on tour and tour related events. It's just a more creative way to live. The last great adventure, in the States, anyway."

Red Beans and Rice
Serves 8

"Cooking is an art, sort of an edible oil painting," explains Jeff. "I'm not very technical about it at all. I just figure out something I want to do and then whatever spices, and I go for it!"

4 cups dry red and/or black beans

2 large white onions, diced

4 cups organic basmati white rice

4 to 5 cups water

4 to 5 cups coconut milk (about 2 cans)

3 cloves fresh garlic, minced (or more)

Fresh basil, to taste

Oregano, to taste

Cumin, to taste

Chili powder, cayenne or red chili peppers, to taste

- Soak the beans for about 24 hours. In a pot, heat the beans gently over the lowest possible heat and then strain. Into a pot, add onions, the beans and uncooked rice along with water and coconut milk.
- Spice to taste. Jeff doesn't measure his spices. His method? "Dump them in until they taste right," he says. Jeff also suggests adding the fresh spices during the last 30 minutes of cooking to keep the taste strong.
- Let the mixture simmer for about 2 hours or until all the water is gone.

In front of Soldier Field in Chicago, Nicholas sits on his blue plastic tarp, observing the burly venue security guards roaming about the parking lot looking to confiscate T-shirts and other familiar tour items.

On this last show of the Dead's 1995 summer tour, Nicholas sells shirts instead of Sabji, a spicy vegetable creation he has made throughout the tour. Sabji, which means vegetable dish, is a steaming mixture of bubbling vegetables and aromatic spices that Nicholas prepares in a huge vat, mixing it with an immense wooden paddle.

Cooking and vending various tour items, Nicholas has been a part of the Grateful Dead scene for years. After graduating from high school in 1988, he packed his car and drove west for tour. There he remained, loving the music and a part of every show until 1991 when he and his partner had a baby.

"I specifically remember thinking to myself, 'I don't know what it is, but I like it,'" says Nicholas of his first experiences. "Having grown up in the typical American suburb, any glimpse of freedom at all is really attractive. At the same time, growing up on the East Coast, the parking lot didn't seem very harsh, where as now, after living on the West Coast for years and years, to come to a place like this is totally disgusting. The first couple of years, before I spent any time settled anywhere, it didn't bother me at all the way beer bottles were up to my knees.

"I'm still here probably because it's like a bad habit. It's a cross between a financial necessity and a junkie's fix or something. I really like the music, and that was what I liked to begin with. The only reason I started vending was because I need to make money to live. Otherwise, I probably wouldn't have bothered. I don't really enjoy it, but I like making food for people. It's definitely a service.

"When I was young, traveling was kind of an experience. It was neat to see different cities and the places in between," he explains. "When you're fresh off the Mom, everything is neat. It's all cool. But after a while, it's not really that cool anymore, because how many nitrous tank people can you argue with in a day? Asking them to please not sell stuff three feet away from your tarp, people are falling on your stuff. It just gets a little much. How many times can you have people take all your stuff, threaten to take you, threaten to take your car. There's so much negative put-down on the scene, that's why all these kids are so scrabbled out with the gangster dank trip, and that's why they're ripping down fences and throwing beer bottles at cops because it's just negative, negative, negative everywhere.

"Between when the Lot opens and when it closes down immediately after the show, the whole time between three and seven, you're scrambling trying to keep out your stuff. Basically what they're creating is a scene where it's easier to walk around selling drugs, than it is to hold up T-shirts, let alone put down a tarp with T-shirts on it.

"For the people who want to do legal stuff, it's a total hassle, which is kind of like the 'Catch 22.' That kinda pisses me off, they're not being responsible to the scene they created. They brought everyone here, everyone is psyched to participate and put energy into the show.

"You're sitting here, trying to be a parcel of higher consciousness, trying to let the people know that 'yes' the sky is blue and it's okay to sit here on a tarp and sell stuff and life doesn't have to be nine to five, and the whole truckin' . . . typical city involved in a typical daydream, hang it up and see what tomorrow brings, but you better not bring a T-shirt to the parking lot because it will get confiscated. So we hang it up, truckin' along, but you're giving us shit every step of the way. That's what I'm frustrated with as far as Grateful Dead land goes. They say the party is because of the vending, but the party isn't because of T-shirts, it's because of the nitrous and beer."

Over the years, Nicholas has embraced Krishna consciousness in the Lot and within himself.

"I got turned on through the music, and what it was I got turned onto was that there is a God. God exists. I was raised agnostic, not that there is or isn't but we're not really participating in any particular church or belief. But through the music and all the people, you get left with no other choice, there is a creator. You come walking out of a show, wake up in the morning, pick up a flower and it's like, who made this? But from the flower to the human body, it's ridiculous to think there's not a creator and once you can accept there is a creator, then it's a total huge step. It's like, 'So, there is a creator, why is He creating, why was I created? What am I supposed to do?' There's a million and one questions. As soon as you make that step from, 'Where is the nitrous tank?' to 'Where is God?' it's like a quantum leap.

"For me it didn't necessarily even happen in Grateful Dead land. I got my first taste at home even before I came to a show, and once I came to a show and experienced the whole thing with a few thousand other people, it's like wow . . . this is pretty overwhelming. So it's kind of like the yin and the yang, because this earth planet is right in the middle of the heavenly planets above and the hellish planets below, and

Nicholas (Sabji-Soul Food).
Photo: Mark Dabelstein

50

Grateful Dead land is the microcosm of the macrocosm; it's the miniature version of the whole world, at least from my perspective. You can find anything you want here, all spectrums of the rainbow. From the total scrabbler junkie guy to a pack of Krishna devotees and everything in between.

"In every city there's always ISKCON (International Society of Krishna Consciousness) devotees that come from the local temple, distributing food and distributing books. Their main purpose here is to distribute the books, the knowledge of Krishna consciousness which basically takes that realization any Deadhead might have that there is a God, the whole 'I am,' estimated thing. The devotees are here with the books to distribute God consciousness because people *here are seeking God* consciousness whether they know it or not.

Sabji-Soul Food
Serves 3 to 5, depending on how hungry you are

Quantities vary depending on what you like. You can use any vegetables. Nicholas maintains it doesn't matter how you slice them, as long as they're the same size.
The following spices are not absolutes. (See Glossary for further spice information. Also, garam masala will encompass many of these spices if you cannot buy them individually)

A few Tbs. ghee or oil (ghee can be bought or made—see Glossary)
1 tsp. cumin seeds
1 tsp. mustard seeds
1 tsp. fennel
1 tsp. coriander
1 tsp. turmeric
Hot pepper to taste
2 tsps. salt
Fresh minced ginger to taste (Nicholas uses 1/3 cup . . . he really likes ginger)

5 medium potatoes, cubed
1 eggplant, cubed
5 fresh tomatoes, diced, or 1 32 oz. can organic ground peeled tomatoes

*Choose one of the following vegetables
1 large zucchini, sliced
1 head broccoli, cut however
1 head cauliflower, cut however

1 to 2 cups basmati rice, cooked

When Nicholas makes Indian food, he begins by dropping spices such as cumin, fennel, coriander and mustard seeds into hot ghee or oil. This draws out the flavor of these aromatic spices. Feel free to use any other spice you feel would complement this dish.

→

- Fry the cumin and mustard seeds (the hard spices) in a skillet with oil or ghee until the seeds start to smoke, pop and crack. Then, throw in the rest of the spices. Next, add fresh minced ginger and allow it to cook slightly. Once the ginger starts to turn brown, add the potatoes. Mix well to evenly coat the potatoes. Cook until the potatoes are partially done and can be poked with a fork.
- Add the eggplant and continue to cook. Once the eggplant is almost soft, add the water. Add enough to steam (probably about 1/2 to 1 cup). This will braise the eggplant and potatoes so they're cooked on the outside but will also draw in the flavor of the spices. When everything starts boiling, cover and continue cooking. Now add the fresh or canned tomatoes.
- Start the rice before adding the soft, steamer vegetables that don't take long to cook (either the zucchini, broccoli or cauliflower). By now, all the hard vegetables should be almost done. Get a feel for how much you want the mixture to cook down. Prepare accordingly. Nicholas tries not to let everything turn into one big mushy soup.
- When done, serve over rice. Careful when eating. This may be spicy!

"The thing that's prime about Grateful Dead land and Rainbow Gatherings and different places where it's hippy dippy and not so much Lollapalooza style, is that a lot of people have already left the norm, they've already given up on what the rest of the world considers reality, and they're searching after absolute truth. The wonderful thing about Dead land is that there's all the different options, there's a billion forks, and it all boils down to what association you keep. You can hang out with the people who are doing the puddles of ecstasy in the hallways, or you can hang out with the people who are totally into organic foods.

"There's all these little mentions in the music that to some might mean, 'You gotta get out there and sell your fat Sammy's (beer) but to others it means, better take this seriously because you never know when this little thing is going to get wrapped up, whether it's tour or the planet earth or just your individual life. People are dying all the time, and that's why the devotees are here, *for who are seeking.* People are like, 'Wow, I love tour, I love freedom, I love the music, I love the party,' and then they get offered all the different options and then because of their karma, their tastes, they choose their own one, you can only go so far down the wrong road before it ends.

"When I was really young, I was faced with all those decisions, now I'm pretty set. I know plenty of people, so even if my car blew up, I'd still be able to get in another one and it wouldn't be weird because I know enough people on tour that it's not a problem. I think that's the cosmic thing about Dead land and why it's going on thirty years later, because it offers all those options at once. Dead land is kind of like the accelerated version of life, it's all so drastic and urgent at all times, no time to lose. The Krishna devotees, they're offering another option.

"Krishna consciousness for me means God consciousness. A lot of people confuse Krishna consciousness as a sectarian thing. Whereas it might have its own dogmas and practices, the application to the masses isn't sectarian at all. It's actually a calling for people to be God conscious. The whole movement is based on chanting in the holy name. The whole process of Krishna consciousness or God consciousness is to remember twenty-four/seven, because basically we don't know when it is we're going to die and that's something that's talked about a lot in music, no time to lose."

Veggie Pot Stickers
Makes 60

Oil (any light oil will do)
Sesame oil
1 onion, diced
5 cloves garlic, minced
1 Tb. firm tofu, mashed with a
  fork
1/2 small red cabbage, shredded
4 carrots, shredded
1 bunch scallions (greens and
  whites), chopped

1 to 2 cups mushrooms, sliced
1 bunch fresh spinach, washed
  and chopped
1 Tb. fresh ginger, minced
1 handful mung beans sprouts
1 package (60 count) Gyoza
  wrappers (these are round,
  vegan dumpling wrappers)

SEASONING
3 Tbs. tamari
1 Tb. teriyaki or vegetarian oyster sauce

Salt and pepper, to taste
Dry mustard, a sprinkle

DIPPING SAUCE
(ALL TO TASTE)
Tamari
Vegetarian oyster sauce

Chile oil
Black pepper
Garlic, minced and to taste

• In a large pot, add oil and sesame oil. When sizzling, add onion
and garlic. Cook for 2 minutes. Add the remaining ingredients.
Season with tamari, salt, pepper, teriyaki or vegetarian oyster sauce
and dry mustard. When the spinach is wilted, remove from heat.
• Into each wrapper add about a tablespoon of filling, wet with a little water to stick, and then fold. In 2 Tbs. light oil and 1 Tb. sesame
oil, cook on a medium-high heat until brown.
• Prepare the dipping sauce and have fun!

Food to Roll With
(a.k.a. Burritos)
❀ ♥ ❀

The Original Fatty Veggie Potato Burrito by the Veggie Sisters

Makes 1 dozen

10 potatoes, cubed
Garlic powder, to taste
Curry, to taste (but theirs always has lots)
Black pepper, to taste
Chili powder, to taste
Seasoning salt, to taste
1 head red cabbage, shredded
1 head green cabbage, shredded
3/4 cup carrots, shredded
3 cups alfalfa sprouts
3 cups bean sprouts
1 dozen 14-inch white flour tortillas
Salsa

- Cube and boil the potatoes (which they say is the hardest part of this process). Drain and mix in the seasonings.
- In a separate bowl, shred the red and green cabbage and the carrots, and mix with the alfalfa and bean sprouts.
- Take two big scoops of the potato mixture and two big handfuls of the vegetable mixture and place down the center of a tortilla. Add salsa (highly recommended by the Veggie Sisters). Wrap in the tortilla and munch. Both Melanie and Steffanie recommend keeping a drink nearby. ("Ask any Deadhead," they say.) It's spicy!

See the Veggie Sisters' homemade candle recipe in the Kind Crafts chapter.

Next to their parking spot in the electric shadows of the Los Angeles Sports Arena an exuberant gathering of Deadheads have formed a drum circle next to where Steffanie and Melanie, (a.k.a. the Veggie Sisters) are cutting vegetables. Set up behind the car they've dubbed their "Touch of Gray" Camaro, Steffanie and Melanie are cooking.

Wearing matching Grateful Dead T-shirts, the two spend their time cutting potatoes, mixing spices and selling their famed Veggie Sister Fatty Potato Burritos, (as well as homemade candles) behind the small, hip-high table they've set up.

"It all started at the summer Las Vegas shows in 1993," explains Melanie. "Basically we were trying out a lot of different things before we got to this recipe. We started out with grilled cheese, broccoli grilled cheese, refried bean burritos, black bean burritos. We were pretty much doing the same thing as everyone else. It was going okay, we were making good money, so we decided to go on tour."

The two made the transition to potato burritos because they couldn't always count on finding black or refried beans in bulk. "On the East Coast, it's so hard to get beans, and that's how it started." Melanie chuckles. "We found that no one else was selling potato veggie burritos. Everybody loved them. From then on we've just been doing the potato veggie burritos."

Spawned from their success on tour, the two were inspired to begin the Veggie Sister business. They create a myriad of assorted crafts, from candles and hair wreaths to jewelry, and sell them in stores near their homes in the Los Angeles area.

"After tour, we started making things at home like candles and jewelry and put them in shops around town," explains Steffanie. "Just sort of a side business. When we went on tour again we made business cards, so we were able to pass them out."

"It's stressful sometimes, but overall, vending is fun," contends Melanie. "You get these things called vending anxiety and parking lot anxiety, and sometimes it's really hard. The anxiety is extremely strong when there is what we call, the 'War on Shakedown' by all the security and staff. The war on Shakedown is crazy. This summer we noticed it like never before. We took pictures of it. It's phenomenal. People were trying to create a Shakedown early in the morning, and the cops were breaking it down. Then, everyone would get in their cars and park somewhere else. They're coming down way too hard on everybody. I mean, everyone is just here to have a good time."

Steffanie and Melanie (Potato Burritos and Candles).
Photo: E. Zipern

Melanie and Steffanie began going to Dead shows in 1989 when they were in high school. Like many Deadheads, the two became interested in the Dead when friends brought them to a show.

"It was just kind of a word-of-mouth type thing," says Melanie. "Friends started telling me about it so I went to a show with them. My first was in Las Vegas. I had a great time. I wasn't vending or anything like that, I was just part of the crowd. I really enjoyed it.

"I love the music," she continues. "For me, it's the atmosphere, the happiness of the whole crowd in there together, just centered on this one thing. It's really, really good. And the energy of it

57

all. A lot of times in the Lot, there are strange vibes going on, really weird stuff. When you're inside the show, it all changes, or so it seems. It's like this one big positive, happy family."

"Not every single time, but I'll go whenever I can," maintains Steffanie. "I mean, I don't center my life around the Grateful Dead. I like to be here, I love the band, it's fun and we make money at it. Two positive things. It's always fun to go inside, and as long as they're playing, it will be a part of my life. Plus, I think they sound good right now."

Melanie and Steffanie especially enjoy going to shows because they are both tremendous Bob Weir fans. Most agree Weir is a talented rhythm guitarist, but fans sometimes belittle him for his "rock star" moves onstage, a style much different from the mellower onstage personas the other band members project. As a result, "Bobby" has been the brunt of many, "Bobby, it ain't easy being cheesy," jokes.

Nonetheless, Melanie and Steffanie love his music and sport an "I've been Weir'd" bumper sticker on the back of their cars. They smile at the thought of him onstage.

"He's so cute." Steffanie giggles.

"Yeah, he's another advantage of the Grateful Dead," adds Melanie. "He's part of that happy, positive feeling that I get."

Rich's Vegan Burritos
Makes 5 to 10 burritos (depending on how fat you make them)

Over the years, Rich's secret to fantastic vegan burritos is with the beans. "I'm proud to say that in my four plus years of vending, I never once used canned beans," he exclaims. "Every burrito is different, so go with the flow, it's kind of all general."

1 pound dry pinto beans, sorted and washed	1 cup brown rice
A few cloves fresh garlic, minced	1/2 head broccoli, cut
1/2 onion, sliced	2 carrots, shredded
Black pepper, salt and cayenne pepper to taste	Whole wheat tortillas
A 4-to-6-inch sprig fresh rosemary (with the stem removed)	Romaine lettuce
	Salsa

• First, all the beans need to be sorted and rinsed. To make this tedious activity more tolerable, Rich fills a white plate or bowl with a few handfuls of dried pinto beans. Then, he picks out dirt particles, small rocks and split or blackened beans.

• Once the beans are picked through, rinse and place in a pot with double the amount of water as beans. Six to 12 hours later when the beans have soaked up most of the water, add more water to cover the beans completely, plus 2 extra inches of water.

• Bring to a boil for 40 to 60 minutes, then lower the heat and cook until tender. While cooking, don't let all the water evaporate or the beans will burn. Keep checking and continually scoop out the foam (which Rich says is caused by gas escaping). Rich says you'll know they're done when you can smash a bean with your finger or a fork and it is mushy. Drain well.

• Once they're cooked, add the garlic, onion, pepper, salt, cayenne and rosemary. Mix well.

• Start the rice. As it cooks, cut the broccoli and shred the carrots. Combine in a bowl. (Rich loves using shredded carrots because it gives a cheeselike look for this vegan delicacy.)

• Though he serves the burrito's vegetable's raw, Rich says you can alter this recipe by sauteing the veggies with fresh garlic. Cook however you like.

• Take a scoop of rice, a scoop of vegetables, a scoop of beans and place in the middle of a whole wheat tortilla. Top with fresh salsa and romaine lettuce, then roll up.

SALSA

1 dozen fresh chopped tomatoes or 1 32 oz. can crushed tomatoes	1 bunch cilantro, minced
1 large onion, diced	1 lemon
2 green peppers, diced	Hot sauce to taste

Amounts will vary depending on vegetable size

• Mix the ingredients together. Pour over the burrito.

It is afternoon on the second of two Grateful Dead shows scheduled at the Knickerbocker Arena in Albany, New York, and people are everywhere on the Shakedown.

Sitting next to Bhakta, an Energy Nugget vendor, Eric is now taking the stationary approach to vending while he sits to rest. From time to time, someone will see his colorful burrito sign and stop to buy one. They're in luck. Of all the possible burritos offered in the Lot, Eric's are specifically designed with a Deadhead's stomach in mind. The rice, corn, pepper, spice mixture is not only vegan, but is also light enough to boogey the night away, dancing inside the show.

"I decided to go with a beanless burrito because it's lighter on my body and I like to spin in the show really hard," explains Eric. "My stomach gets upset if I have heavy food in it, so I thought that there are other people out there who dance really hard and want to have the food in them to do that, so I didn't use the beans, and I tried to go all the way organic.

"It's related to the Grateful Dead," he continues. "I think food holds a lot of energy, so you want it to be a positive thing, not something that you're all angry when you're making. And I do vegan so I can appeal to everybody on the Lot. I was vegan myself and know the whole struggle with it sometimes because it's not a limiting diet, but it's limiting as compared to the way our society puts food out."

Eric (Veggie Rice Burrito).
Photo: Mark Dabelstein

Though he doesn't remember much of the occasion, Eric's first show was with his father when he was eight years old at the Baltimore Civic Center, in Maryland. Little did he know that years later, the Dead scene would become his second home and by 1995, his show totals would reach 150.

"My dad is not into the Dead but he's into all the music from the late sixties, so when they were in town, we went," remembers Eric. "He had backstage passes and I got to sit on Jerry's lap backstage as an eight-year-old, and all of them signed the back of my T-shirt. My mother washed it, so I have this 1980 tour shirt with all their autographs that my mom washed. It took all the autographs out. But at the time I hated it. I remember being there and it just seemed like the longest four hours, it was so boring and dull, but six years later, I find myself here again, loving it!

"When I came back, my impression was that this is the greatest place on earth, the greatest music, the people. I was definitely naive to a lot of things that I'm hip to now, but I wanted to be a part of it. I was in a rebellious stage, I wanted to fit in and I wanted to be part of this because it felt like a place that I didn't have to be angry at the world and just be here and be conscious.

60

"I was definitely a critical Deadhead. I'd go in and listen note for note, and I'd look for those peak performance shows where all the notes were in the right place and Jerry's voice was sounding perfect. Now that I just go in and dance the whole show, I'm less critical of it and I'm just appreciative. I'm doing healing. That's why I'm here. When I'm dancing, I get pretty emotional. A lot of stuff that's going on in my life is reflecting on the music, just going through experiences in my past. So when I'm dancing, it's definitely a healing process. It's therapy and the vibrations of music just hit exactly the right chord in me and help me to move, like it's driving me. I haven't found other music that does that like this. Reggae can do it at the right times, but nothing like this.

"Spinning is a big part of it for me, specifically because it's more of a meditation. I'm really glad that I found that form of meditation, because it really does a lot. It's totally high. I've tried a few different types of meditation and it didn't work for me. I really hadn't thought about working out stuff in my life before either, and then I found that I could start working things out through dancing and that it would open me up. It makes me happy, it makes me feel good, and it makes me feel more open to other people too. This summer has been an incredible thing, I've been in every show since the tour started and that's a first for me, to go in to every show and get the full picture of the music and what's happening. It's been great and I've connected with more people on this trip.

"I think it has a lot to do with the fact that I'm in there, taking the show in more of a spiritual space, and looking at it as a meditation. I have more respect for the whole thing, the Grateful Dead and the people. I praise the music and I praise the people here."

Eric's Fantastic Veggie Rice Burrito
* Serves 4 *

*All ingredients (especially vegetables) should be organic.

1 1/2 cups long and/or short grain rice
1 cup frozen corn, thawed
1 cup yellow onion, diced chunky
1/2 cup red sweet onions, diced chunky
1 green bell pepper, cut in long thin strips, then chopped
1 red bell pepper, cut in little squares

A pinch of jalapeno pepper, minced
1 cup salsa (The salsa adds flavor and keeps the mixture moist, which is great for mixing)
1 tsp. chili powder
1 tsp. garlic powder
1 cubanel pepper, sliced
4 fat-free whole wheat tortillas

• Prepare the rice and let cool. Then, chop the vegetables and mix together with the rice, salsa and spices (the veggies will be raw).
• Place a heaping spoonful of the mixture in the middle of a tortilla. Roll up and enjoy.

Since they moved to Telluride a few years back, Stephen, Shawn, Chantal, David and David's sister, Christina, have made a habit of trekking west every summer to the yearly desert Dead shows in Las Vegas. It is a run that every year David swears he won't do, but always goes anyway. To pay for their travels during the summer of '95 shows, the five cooked up organic burritos with tempeh.

"We just piled up into Chantal and Christina's Volkswagen buses and drove across the desert from southwest Colorado to the fifth annual Vegas Dead shows," recalls David. "I've been to all five years, Christina had been to like four of them, and Stephen has been to two, so it's kind of like an annual trip, and the vending scene is always so huge in Vegas.

"I think we were all into it because it gave us a focus instead of just going to the shows and hanging out in the heat. It was like, 'This year, let's go and provide some really good food.' We decided to do it organic and vegan because we figured that there are enough people now in 1995 that really want that energy. There's a lot of good food at the show, but there's also a lot of shwagy food that you just don't want to eat. We wanted to provide an organic and vegan option. I think we were pretty pleased with what we came out with."

"We got the idea for this about a month before the shows, and David works in an organic store, The Natural Source in Telluride," adds Shawn. "So he and Stephen got it all together as for the concept of tempeh instead of just beans and rice."

"For me, it was a really high experience," explains Stephen. "I knew I was going to catch a show or two and I knew I wanted to sell really good high-quality food that was going to keep people healthy. I've been cooking for a few years now and I'm really into good food and I knew that there was a real need for good food. There are people who will seek you out for that kind of quality, care and love put into food.

"It was surprising how everything did fall together for us. A lot of different people helped out in different ways. It was such a high time and everything that fell around at the concert was amazing—the way it came together from the first night all the way through to getting the food prepared and getting it sold."

Both David and Stephen roughed out the weather because they knew the Vegas shows meant meeting up with old friends who live throughout the West Coast.

"It was an incredible experience, because there were a lot of people that I knew there," says Stephen. "I felt a sense of connectedness with friends outside of where we were living, as well as with other friends we knew on the Dead scene who would be there, coming from California, other parts of Colorado, Arizona or wherever. It was sort of a converging point for a lot of different friends out West to go there."

A few years after discovering the Dead's music, David began traveling to as many shows as he could drive to. Going to school in Dallas, Texas, made the traveling difficult, but he was hooked.

"It blew me away," says David. "I had a copy of the *Official Book of the Deadheads,* and all the pictures in there were like what the parking lot was like—in color and real. Growing up in Memphis, then going to School in Dallas, it's like you just don't see hippies. They're just very conservative places to live. When we pulled into the parking lot, it was young hippies en masse walking around. It was what I always wanted, but had never been offered. All of a sudden it was there and I was psyched.

"From then on, I was just psyched. Getting to the point of my last shows, they were just personal experiences. Every Dead show was usually some turning point in my life or during a very important time in my life, and always served as a catharsis to go to a show and be in that energy. You could always run away and go to a show when there was nowhere else to go.

Righteous Tempeh Burritos, Always Vegan
Makes 6 to 8 Burritos

2 cups brown rice
15 oz. can refried beans
Oil or margarine (to saute with)
8 oz. package tempeh, chopped
1 medium carrot, sliced (any vegetables will work. Try broccoli, squash, kale, celery)
1 red onion, sliced
1 green pepper, sliced
8 to 12 cloves garlic (or to taste), minced
Salt to taste
1 1/2 to 2 Tbs. chili powder
1 to 1 1/2 Tbs. cumin
Cayenne to taste
2 good pinches black pepper
12 oz. can tomato puree or sauce
1 small handful cilantro, chopped
8 to 10 tortillas
1 pint sprouts (any kind, but alfalfa works great)
100% Love. . . Add liberally throughout the dish!

- In separate pots, cook the rice and then the beans. Set both pots aside.
- Saute the chopped tempeh, carrot, onion and green pepper in oil or margarine until soft. Add garlic and all the spices while the vegetables saute.
- Add the tomato puree or sauce and bring to a simmer for 10 minutes, then add the cilantro. It should look like a chili, so if it is too watery, cook longer. In a tortilla, place some of the rice, beans and tempeh-vegetable-spice mixture and top with sprouts.

"Dead shows have completely affected my life," he continues. "They have a lot to do with why I think the way I think about a lot of things, where I'm at and the path that I'm on. The Grateful Dead are a humongous influence on my life, and just about everyone I know."

"I was really in awe, I didn't know what to think, it was just so strange that this existed," remembers Stephen. "I went to a pretty straight prep school, and I couldn't believe that this happened. I think the first few experiences or more, I was more a voyeur than a participator because it was so far removed from any experience that I ever had. I didn't know how to inter-act, what I found was that it didn't matter how I interacted as long as I came with an open heart. I really didn't know how to dance either. And so I realized that it didn't matter if I did or not. I had danced before, don't get me wrong, I grew up in the seventies so I was well acquainted with disco but this certainly wasn't disco, at all.

"The music is inspirational, if nothing else. It creates a sense of connectedness amongst a large group of individuals in which the sum of the experience is greater than the parts of the individuals that were there, I mean, no individual could ever re-create that experience. Really, it's superb."

Darrin and Mark (Bad Mo Fo Veggie Burrito).
Photo: Mark Dabelstein

Darrin and Mark live in Knoxville, Tennessee, a state that the Dead don't play in very often. When the '95 shows in Memphis were announced, the two were thrilled. Mark had always wanted to go to a show, and Darrin wanted to be the one to take him.

"I just recently started listening to them a couple of years ago. I never had the chance to go to a show, so I finally got off my duff and went to the shows in Memphis," says Mark. "It blew me away. You have so many people from so many different walks of life, it just blew me away how everything went so peacefully, how everything works out so smooth, the conglomeration of people. And that was the thing about it. What are all these people here for? What is going on? Once I got in the show and heard them live, I realized.

"When Jerry wailed, I've never had goose bumps running through my body like that before," he continues. "It's the way they do their music. I've never seen it go through a group of people and make a groove in such a way. And the way they play to an audience, the way they speak to their music, how they pay attention to their fans, that's something else. The music is the main thing, it spans out, so far, touches so many different aspects of my life, and that was all it took. It took one show, it's the only thing I've ever done in my life once and been automatically hooked."

Bad Mo Fo Veggie Burrito
Makes 4 burritos

1 cup dry black beans, soaked and cooked
1 cup chili beans (about 1/2 a can)
1/2 tsp. cumin
1 Tb. garlic powder
1/2 tsp. coriander
1/2 tsp. chili powder
A pinch cayenne
1 cup organic brown rice
4 12-inch whole wheat tortillas
1/2 cup cheddar cheese, shredded
1/2 cup Monterey Jack cheese, shredded
1 cup Georgia vidalia onion, chopped (a sweet, white onion)
1 cup shredded lettuce
1 cup salsa

- After cooking the black beans, add the chili beans, spices and let simmer. Mark says the longer they simmer, the better.
- While it simmers, start the rice.
- To build the burrito, place the following ingredients in the center of a tortilla. For each burrito, add in the following order:

  1/4 cup cooked brown rice
  1/4 cup bean mixture
  1/4 cup Monterey Jack and cheddar cheese
  1/4 cup chopped onion
  1/4 cup shredded lettuce
  1/4 cup salsa

- "Then, roll that fatty up and eat," says Mark.

Unbeknownst to Darrin, after his first show in Memphis, Mark grabbed ingredients to make quesadillas from the restaurant where he cooks and took off for the next scheduled shows in Birmingham, Alabama, without Darrin. Now they laugh about how hooked Mark really was, but Darrin understands.

"That's what it did to me." agreed Darrin. "It bit me like that. You see one and boom, you're suckered. It was so funny to see a very dear friend of mine who I never would have expected. It was really cool to see him immediately back at it. He's taken it a step further. It happened to me, hell, it happens to all of us. We are everywhere."

So three months later, Darrin and Mark took off from their jobs as chefs in Knoxville and followed the tour starting in Michigan, all the way to the last show in Chicago. The two made gourmet burritos called, Bad Mo Fo Burritos. But the venture didn't come without some sacrifices.

"Hell, I sold my car to go on tour, I've been walking everywhere." Mark laughs now. "It meant that much to me. And the food aspect was great, because that's what I do. You were there in every different city, cooking and enjoying putting out good food for people. I enjoyed doing a good product, I like feeding people, I love making food. You got to meet everybody, then you see them in the next city. It was a way to get to the next town, but you also felt like you were contributing something."

Darrin's first show was in 1987, though he was introduced to their music years before that.

"One Halloween evening, under the influence of many things, one of my best friends from many years ago turned me onto 'Dead Set,'" recalls Darrin. "I was truly fascinated with 'Franklin's Tower.' After sitting with the cows, in a big pasture, watching the sunrise and listening to that album over and over again, I was like, 'It's time to go to a show.' And we went and saw some shows. I remember asking my mother to write me a note so that I could get out of school to see shows. She said, 'I kinda figured that you were all into that lifestyle.' I did my first tour that year.

"The funny thing was that I fell in love with the Grateful Dead years before I fell in love with food. There are four things in my life that I love equally. Food and the Grateful Dead are two of them.

"One of my favorite quotes is, 'The Dead are like an empty pitcher, we fill them up with our energy, and they fill us up with their music.' I mean thousands of people, the energy, the groove, the music. . . and the music. Wow! I remember a New Years Eve show, three feet from the speaker. I don't think I opened my eyes once, I know I didn't. You can actually feel the music in each little cell, it just gets down inside ya, and you can't get it out."

When the Dead came back to the Seattle Memorial Stadium on their 1995 summer tour, Stephanie Glazerman and friends traveled to the shows by ferry; a twenty-minute ride from their homes on Vashon Island in the Puget Sound. Stephanie loves to cook, so she financed the trip by vending a favorite chickpea creation, Chickpea Chapatis.

"I did it just for fun, and I'm also kinda underemployed at the moment," she says, laughing. "I had time, so I figured, what the hell? It's just nice to have something to trade."

Though she has never traveled throughout a full tour, Stephanie tries to catch Dead shows whenever she can and has seen them all over the country. Her first was at the Worcester Centrum in 1983. She loves the scene and takes every opportunity to be in it.

"The band and the crowd are independent, but they stimulate creativity in each other, and that's a special relationship that's kept the Grateful Dead family going for all these years," observes Stephanie. "Grateful Dead Land is a bizarre culture, totally open, creative and outrageous. If only the bliss of the scene weren't tainted by Ticketron and other unfortunate weirdness of our modern (un)civilization."

Stephanie (Chef Stef's Chickpea Chapatis).
Photo: E. Zipern

In recent years, cooking has become a passion for Stephanie. As she learns more about sustainable agriculture and natural resources, she finds that cooking is a way to celebrate the cycle of life.

"Cooking has been a really rewarding creative outlet for me and it's also been a challenge, too, since it relates to a lot of bigger issues in the rest of the world like health and natural resources. I feel sensitive to a lot of that stuff. It's been interesting trying to evolve my own diet into something that's a little more to my values, or my ideal world that I imagine.

"I'm trying to think more about getting food locally and in season, organically grown and in bulk," she says. "All those things have to do with resources and energy and how you can create beautiful food out of what's around you. That's one of the amazing things about living here, in a land of abundance. Right now it's blackberry season. Eating for sustainability is really what we need to evolve toward."

On the island, Stephanie and her housemates have gardens, blackberry bushes and lots of open land to run with their dogs. This summer Stephanie has worked hard on creating her own garden.

"I've had gardens before, but this is my first solo garden. It's kind of been a work in progress and a learning experience that is fun and feels great. I wish I were better at it." She laughs.

Stephanie has a clear view of her garden whenever she emerges from her home, a 10-foot-by-12-foot tent that is situated a good distance from the main house where the kitchen is. Heavy, off-white canvas covers a wood platform that holds her bed, books and assorted belongings. Next to the tent, she can lie in the hammock tied to a madrona tree and relax with stretches of green forest everywhere behind her.

"In the wintertime I had a little wood burning stove with two propane burners," she explains. "I hear owls at night and pheasants cackling as they walk around. The path to the house goes through the blackberries and the garden space.

Chef Stef's Chickpea Chapatis
Serves at least 6

A few tsps. light oil
1 large onion, chopped
A good amount of garlic, minced
2 (or more) tsps. finely grated ginger
2 cups chopped vegetables (peppers or whatever you have around)
1 Tb. each, cumin, coriander, turmeric, garam masala, paprika
A dash of cayenne

1 1/2 cups crushed tomatoes (about 1 15 oz. can)
4 cups chickpeas (a.k.a. garbanzo beans), soaked, cooked and drained (about 2 cans if you don't have dry)
1 to 2 cups stock or water (to prevent sticking)
A splash of lemon juice
A bunch of cilantro, chopped
Enough chapatis for your hungry friends

• In a deep kettle, saute the onions in oil over medium heat. When they become soft and translucent, add garlic, ginger and the chopped vegetables, starting with the hardest ones first.
• After a few minutes, (but before the vegetables become too soft) add the spices, followed by the crushed tomatoes and cooked chickpeas.
• Cover, turn down the flame and let the flavors harmonize for the next 30 to 40 minutes, with an occasional stir and adding extra stock or water if necessary to avoid sticking. Taste and adjust the seasoning. Top off with a splash of lemon juice and chopped cilantro before rolling in chapatis. Stef suggests adding extra vegetables (like something green and steamed, raw or chopped) for texture and flavor.

"It feels really good to be breathing outside air, though I'm not breathing it all the time, because I spend a lot of the time in the house, in the kitchen and with the piano. There's a lot of people in that house, which is great because it's a real family, but it's also nice to have a sanctuary and have some quiet space. I couldn't ask for a better place to be right now."

On a sunny, dusty, people-packed Shakedown, Amanda stands in a long skirt, holding a wicker basket filled with tinfoil rolled Rice Veggie Wraps. Before traveling to the Portland show, Amanda knew she would have to sell something to pay for her trip. She chose food for the service she can provide.

"Cooking food is one of my favorite services," she explains. "To cook organic and vegan food, to provide that for people who want the best for their bodies, for their temples.

"Service is where you find joy and fulfillment in giving to others and giving for the greater community," continues Amanda. "In order to work on ourselves, we need to lose ourselves, and by doing service for others, for the greater good, then we can perfect our individual selves. It's all the same interconnected web giving positive energy on one level that affects all levels. The universe is a mandala, a hologram in which each part mirrors everything else. Our individual bodies are mirrors for the planetary bodies, whether we choose to be aware of it or not.

"In astrology there's one house which describes where you find your most fulfilling service, the house of Virgo. I have Cancer on my sixth house cusp, and my most fulfilling service is doing Cancer type activities; mothering and nurturing and healing, healing with food, herbs, ayurveda and changing consciousness.

Rice and Veggie Wrap with Tahini Dressing
Serves 4

*All ingredients should be organic.
1 1/2 cups brown rice
2 carrots, chopped large
1 bunch kale, chopped
1 large head broccoli, cut in small florets
1/4 cup toasted sunflower seeds
4 whole wheat chapatis or tortillas

TAHINI DRESSING
Juice of 1 lemon
1/2 cup tahini
Garlic to taste, (but she recommends using at least 3 cloves)
1/2 cup water (or more to thin)
Tamari to taste

• Start the rice. While that cooks, chop and steam the vegetables.
• Once the rice is done, combine in a large bowl with the sunflower seeds and steamed vegetables.
• Prepare the tahini dressing and mix well. Pour over the rice and vegetables and mix together. Fill the chapatis with the mixture, roll and eat.

**Extra sauce can be prepared to dip into or just have around.

"Part of my work on this planet is to study astrology. It describes what is, it helps you to go with your own flow, to do what you're naturally good at. It shows where the different archetypal energies manifest in your life. It's the cosmic science, the only science that I'll deal with.

"What a lot of people don't understand about healing is that when problems arise externally in your life, it's a sign that you're ignoring something on the inside. This is what esoteric healing is all about. Every vibration you put out determines what kind of energy comes back to you.

"A lot of us have come home to our spiritual family through the Grateful Dead scene. We are a family of souls who feel this innate pull to become spiritual selves. The shows could sometimes be that ecstatic ritual ceremony. Somehow going to church fails to give our generation what we need—to be shaken in awe by the eternity and oneness of the spirit. And we found it by getting high on the music together."

Amanda (Rice and Veggie Wrap). Photo: E. Zipern

In a tiny rented apartment in Boston's North End, Deborah and Catherine live while they work and go to school in the Boston area. When the summer hits, the two take every opportunity to get away. Traveling to Highgate, Vermont, for the annual summer shows scheduled there gets them out of the city and driving north to see the Grateful Dead.

The 1995 shows scheduled in the remote Vermont town were a destination for Catherine, Deborah, and their friend Richard, who went to his first show there. The three spent the five-hour trip north listening to music and making signs for the organic vegetable roll ups they were selling.

"We both live in the North End and we wanted to escape, get off to the country," says Deborah. "For me, I just wanted to sell and maybe we'd make enough to pay for our trip there and back to Boston. The best part was walking around, selling them. I remember going to my first show and finding some of the great food that was there. I really appreciated it. I wanted to share that feeling and I knew people would want real organic veggies.

"Making the veggie roll ups was the best thing," she continues. "I met so many people, just had a great weekend, escaped the city. We stayed outside the fairgrounds the first night, had a big campfire, hung out with friends, cooked good food and had a really great time. It was a really nice escape, it was great, but I wasn't expecting that many people at Highgate. I didn't realize how huge it was; it did shock me. The only time I didn't like it was getting in and out of the show, but all in all I enjoyed it."

"It was great, the energy started right away," explains Catherine. "We were on the highway and getting closer and closer and getting excited. Richard got a kick out of that because

Organic Veggie Roll Up
Serves 4

4 whole wheat or sprouted wheat tortillas
Lots of hummus per sandwich (They bought their hummus and added lemon juice, cayenne, pepper and salt, but feel free to make your own.)
2 carrots, shredded
Green leaf lettuce
2 tomatoes, sliced
A few fresh basil leaves, minced or whole
Any other spare organic vegetables you feel like putting in

• Catherine, Deborah and Richard bought a bunch of organic vegetables to put their roll ups together. Take a tortilla and stuff it with hummus, carrots, lettuce, tomatoes, basil leaves and anything else you want to throw in.

he didn't realize how many people were going to be there. We camped on Lake Champlain, which was so beautiful; we had a full moon right on the lake. We met so many cool people. It was just so nice and relaxing. Then the next day we came to the show, we camped in the airport and a different kind of fun began, it was great. It was Richard's first show, and he was completely blown away, he loved it. He was overwhelmed by the sense of community. It was really nice to turn somebody on to that who had never experienced it before.

"I look so forward to the Highgate shows all year. Just working with school and not having much free time, it's just bliss and heaven once we get out to Vermont," she adds. "I've always liked the Dead. I love the scene, I love the dancing, and just anything goes, especially in Vermont. It's nice to be around so many kindred spirits who are all there for mostly the same thing."

Lynn (Vegan Spring Rolls). Photo: Mark Dabelstein

If her hands aren't wet from dunking rice paper into a small sliver bowl filled with water, they are covered with pieces of spring roll filling. Lynn is moving quickly behind her table, rushing to immerse the rice paper in water, laying it out on tinfoil, filling the thin, white, round paper with vegetable mixture and then tightly rolling it up.

In between announcing that the Spring Rolls with Thai Peanut Sauce are ready, Lynn darts in and out of her rig, a '73 Dodge Diamond RV, to mix the famed, secret Thai peanut sauce which everyone raves about.

Over the years, Lynn has sold scores of the usual tour items, but the Spring Rolls are her current offering. People can't get enough of them. They often return to compliment her on a difficult dish to prepare anywhere, let alone on Grateful Dead tour. Lynn loves making the Spring Rolls for their energy and the service she is providing.

"I feel there are five highs in life," says Lynn with conviction, demonstrating with her five outstretched fingers. "One is your friends, they're the thumb which makes everything else in the hand worthwhile, because if you have no one to share with, it's absolutely nothing at all. Two, is food, because no matter what you do, you've got to have it. Third, music, is the universal language we can communicate with each other through. The fourth, of course which we all know is beer and buds, you gotta have that, they're the great things in life. Party favors, we all have them. And the fifth, making love, sharing with another individual that which you have within yourself, is least on the list, so that's where the food comes in.

"When you eat good food you become one with the energy of the earth, that which is around you. You're taking into your body the energy that exists in another living being, putting it within your own to create a oneness, not only with yourself and the world around you, but with the universe beyond, because it's all relative. The only thing different between me and this rice paper that I'm laying on this tinfoil is the way that our molecules are put together. It's just as alive as I am, but in a different sense. Like the peanut sauce. When I make the peanut sauce I focus only on the peanut sauce, that's all I think about when I make it. Like the garlic, it's not just garlic anymore, it's garlic in Thai peanut sauce. It needs to have a little time to adapt to the fact that it's becoming one with everything else around it to create another individual living being. The Thai peanut sauce is very alive, it breathes, it moves, it's crazy, it's wild, it really is."

At sixteen, Lynn became a vegetarian and began cooking for herself. She grew up in a family that ate, "really shwag food."

"Franco-American, Kraft and Chef Boyardee, pork chops and steaks and those kind of gross, disgusting things. In order for me to survive in that house when I was still in high school, I had to learn how to cook, otherwise I would have starved to death. They definitely couldn't provide what I wanted to eat, so I made my own food."

For the last three years, Lynn has been going to shows and traveling around the country in her rig. The large vehicle is Lynn's home and it offers her many more possibilities than simply journeying in a car.

"I love it. Do you know how many times the Grateful Dead have played in my backyard?" She laughs. "It's really nice, though it's a lot of work to do my own auto mechanics and cook food on tour. It really is a big amount of energy, but the reality is, it goes back to the energy thing. Nothing is yours until you pass it on to another, I truly believe that. It's the same as my home. My door is always open. I just believe in that because that's the energy I choose to live my life in and it always comes back to me so nicely. I love being a part of it; it's really exciting for me.

"There is nothing like a Jerry jam. It's crazy . . . it makes me laugh, it makes me so excited. I tell myself I'm sick of it, I don't need it, I want to get away, I'm tired of the scene, so I go away from it for a month and a half, and God, I can't wait to go to a show again. It's crazy, I've seen well over two hundred shows. I don't come here to make money in the parking lot. I come here to see the Grateful Dead. And when I don't get in and I sit in the parking lot, a lot of times I'll cry. I want to be inside, I want to dance because the music is so beautiful. Because when you look at the energy of everything every sound has a color, so I take myself to this place that is all color, all light, so beautiful, like God. Music is a universal language, and for

Vegan Spring Rolls

Makes a bunch. Prepare to feed lots of friends and the occasional passerby

NOTES

*These will keep for up to three hours wrapped in foil or wax paper in the fridge.

*Anything that sounds out of the ordinary can be purchased at an Oriental market or health food store.

*The Thai Peanut Sauce needs to chill for 24 hours, so take that into account before you start.

*A thought from Lynn as you cook . . . "The love of kind food is a light of life!"

THE ROLL

1 16 oz. package rice noodles

Carrots, shredded

Equal parts red and green cabbage, shredded

Mung bean sprouts

2 to 3 Tbs. olive oil

1 Tb. sesame oil

8 oz. mock duck, sliced (also referred to as wheat gluten, or seitan—see Glossary)

1 pound of firm tofu, cut in 1/2-inch cubes

1 1/2 Tb. curry powder

1/2 sprig lemon grass, chopped fine (also found in bulk)

3 Tbs. fresh grated ginger

3 to 4 Tbs. red chili paste

1 bulb of garlic, peeled and chopped fine

A handful of fresh basil, chopped fine

1 8 oz. package rice paper

"This is something that you just have to work with," says Lynn. "It is by far the most particular food product I've ever worked with. It needs to be in the water for the exact amount of time and you need to wrap it in the exact amount of time or it turns rubbery. There is a Zen to rolling a rice paper, you gotta get into the groove with it, you gotta be 'one' with it. That's my trick. I do think it's a thing of love. I put lots of love and energy in each and every one."

• To cook the rice noodles, get the water boiling, then turn it off. Add the noodles and let soak for 2 or 3 minutes. Expect them to be rubbery and firm—not quite al dente. Pull them out and let sit for another minute. In a colander, pour cold water over them until chilled. Set aside.

• Mix the vegetables together.

• In a medium to large saute pan, heat the olive and sesame oil. Add the mock duck, tofu, curry powder, lemon grass, ginger, chili paste and however much garlic your palate desires. Saute until lightly browned. Add basil. Saute 2 to 3 more minutes, remove from heat and let cool in fridge.

→

• When all the ingredients are cooled, fill a large bowl with room temperature water. Place the rice paper into the water one at a time. (Don't let more than six sit in there at a time, and remember, practice makes perfect.)

• Remove when slightly soggy and lay flat on the counter to roll. Place a small amount of the noodles, the vegetables, and the spice mixture in the center of the rice paper and roll.

1. Lay out flat (Diagram A)
2. Fold the two end sides toward the center (Diagram B)
3. Flip bottom up (Diagram C)
4. Roll upward (Diagram D)

*Tip—Don't pick the roll up until stage 4 is complete, or it will rip.

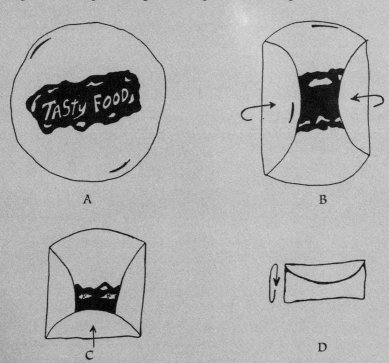

Thai Peanut Sauce

1 to 3 cups water (not cold, just room temperature)
2 cups chunky unsalted peanut butter
1/2 cup peanut/sesame oil mixture. Mix the oil in a 2-to-1 ratio (more peanut than sesame). The
   amount of oil can also be reduced to 1/3 cup.
2 Tbs. rice vinegar
1 cup honey or fructose
Juice of 1 1/2 lemons
1/2 sprig lemon grass, finely chopped
2 to 3 Tbs. grated ginger (more or less as desired)
1/4 cup chili paste
1/4 bunch cilantro, finely chopped
Lots of garlic, to taste

- Mix the water into the peanut butter *slowly* to create a semithick paste.
- Add oil, vinegar, honey and lemon juice. Stir together.
- Add all the spices and stir. Thin out with more water until you have a creamy consistency.
- Cover. Let sit in fridge, "chillin'" for 24 hours. Sauce will thicken, thin with water as necessary.
Dip the spring rolls into the sauce and enjoy!

*Note—This sauce can also be used on pasta and sandwiches. Be creative. If you add more oil and
vinegar, it makes a great salad dressing.*

me, dance is the voice through which I speak. I love dancing, and there's no band, no music in
the whole wide world that does to my body what the Grateful Dead does to my body and I
love it because I let go and I let be."

It is 11 A.M., and the temperature and humidity have already risen to new, intolerable levels outside Soldier Field, Chicago's sports arena alongside Lake Michigan. Next to Ayleen and Diana's barbecue, the heat is even more intense.

The two sit next to the scorching barbecue so they can continue placing burritos on the grill. Behind them hangs a bright, swirling, yellow, red and orange flag, which Ayleen made last year. Printed upon it is a reminder, *Keep on the Sunny Side.*

Ayleen and Diana are each other's oldest friends. They've been friends since the third grade but as September rolls around, they will go their separate ways again. Ayleen to study photography in Ireland and Diana for her second year at the University of Missouri. For now, the two are happy to be at this Chicago show together cooking burritos.

Keep on the Sunny Side Tortillas
* Serves 6 *

"It's very important to cook a lot, and not be intimidated by cooking," says Ayleen. "Experimenting and being confident in your cooking can result in some wonderful meals. Cook with friends. Enjoy being and feeding the body well."

1/2 head broccoli, diced
1 zucchini, sliced
A bunch of large, fat mushrooms, sliced
2 cups cooked black beans (approximately 1 15 oz. can)
2 cups cooked kidney beans (approximately 1 15 oz. can)
Sharp cheddar cheese, shredded and sprinkled to taste (She doesn't use very much, just enough to hold it all together.)
1 cup salsa
1 cup sour cream
6 tortillas

• Ayleen recommends you buy vegetables on sale. This recipe is extremely interchangeable with a plethora of fresh vegetables. "If mushrooms are on sale that week, then load it up with mushrooms," she says.
• The amount of vegetables used is really according to your taste. Steam the cut broccoli and zucchini and then saute the mushrooms. In a bowl, combine the steamed vegetables and mushrooms with the beans, cheese, salsa and sour cream. Mix well.
• Place a scoop of the mixture in the center of a tortilla and wrap well by folding the bottoms inward and the sides up.
• Wrap each tortilla, then heat on a barbecue, in a skillet, oven grill, toaster. Anything that will crisp it. Cook until heated and the tortilla has become crispy.

Ayleen's creation, Keep on the Sunny Side Tortillas, is a crispy tortilla, stuffed with vegetables, beans, salsa, sour cream and cheese. It began years ago when Ayleen wanted to eat with her family but keep a vegetarian diet.

"It started out because my family was always making chicken burritos and I didn't eat meat so I kinda invented my own things that I could eat along with them," she explains. "My mom always wanted us to eat the same things instead of making a totally different meal when we would have family meals, so I invented my own little version of something that would be good and simple."

Before the afternoon began, Ayleen's creation quickly sold out. The two were happy to hang out and meet people. Ayleen also brought homemade candles and photographs of flowers and plants she has taken over the years.

"I was going to bring a camera," says Ayleen. "I love taking pictures of people. What I love is images of people and people enjoying themselves, doing peopley things. People photos are just incredible. I could sit and look at people photos all day.

"One of my goals in life is to meet as many people as I can, talk with as many people as I can, and being down here, it's really easy," she continues. "Everyone is in a good mood, everyone is smiling, it's a beautiful day out, there's music . . . its just like a big festival. I don't even necessarily think that it has to be that the Grateful Dead is playing, it's just the fact that everyone comes together for an event. But the music is happy music, easygoing music. It's mellow at times, it's rockin' at times, but it's not offensive, not angry. It's got a good feel."

"All my friends where I live listen to the Dead," explains Diana. "They're very big fans. I asked them, 'Would I like it?' They said, it's just the nicest, most chilled out thing in the world, relaxing all day and then going in to dance, so I figured, what's not to like about that?"

Between the Bunz

❀ ❤ ❀

A strange coincidence indeed. Erin Beltz didn't plan on going to her first Dead show, nor did she imagine leaving Minnesota and moving to California a year later. At a 1993 show in Chicago (her first), Erin met her boyfriend, Joey, and later moved to his reservation in Northern California. Now she has a job she loves and lives in a lush environment many would envy.

"I had listened to the Dead before, but I mostly went because I was working at a restaurant as a waitress and some friends came in late one night and said they were going to Chicago to go see the Grateful Dead," remembers Erin. "I had never seen the Grateful Dead before and I had never been to Chicago, so I was like, 'I'll go!' And then I met him." She smiles, motioning toward Joey in the back of their 1976 dirty banana-colored Volkswagen bus.

To finance their trip to the 1994 December shows in Oakland, Erin and Joey sold a number of delectable sandwiches, the Trim Reaper and the Sgt. Pepper's Lonely Pineapple Clubwich.

The Trim Reaper
Serves 2

2 slices of 9 or 13 grain bread (or any good bread)
Apple butter, to taste
1/4 carrot, grated
1/4 celery stalk, grated
3 thin slices of pear
A few tsps. sunflower seeds, to taste

• Erin says the sandwich is dubbed the Trim Reaper because it's good for you. Spread apple butter on both slices of the bread. Next, place the grated carrot on one slice of the bread and the grated celery on the other. The apple butter will help the celery and carrots stick to the bread.
• Add the pear slices and sprinkle sunflower seeds to taste. Close the sandwich and enjoy!

*See Erin's yummy recipe for Sweet Treats in the How Sweet It Is chapter!

"We usually don't make much money, just enough so we can get here and get home and have fun," explains Erin. "We end up giving half of our stuff away at the end of the day."

Joey and Erin both tutor tribal children on the Hoopa Valley Indian Reservation, in Humboldt County, California. There, Joey is a member of the Hupa Valley tribe. Fifty miles east of Eureka, the Hupa Valley is a quiet, sparsely populated community alongside the Klamath and Trinity rivers. It's all nestled under tall, green majestic mountains that can be seen from around the valley.

"I like it, not having anything to do," says Erin. "That's kinda why I went there. I knew there wouldn't be anything to do and I'd have time to do things I wanted to do, instead of getting caught up in going to bars or just hanging out with friends for twelve years and realizing, 'Man, none of us ever did anything.'

Sergeant Pepper's Lonely Pineapple Clubwich
Serves 2

2 pieces of any good quality light bread
2 large lettuce leafs (helps to keep the bread from getting soggy)
2 hot peppers (hot is key!), fresh, canned or jarred
1 to 2 slices mozzarella cheese (or soy cheese)
1 slice fresh or canned pineapple

• On one slice of bread, place a piece of lettuce. On top of that add the hot peppers, the cheese, and then the pineapple. Add another piece of lettuce and top with the second slice of bread. Enjoy!

Joey and Erin (Sergeant Pepper's Lonely Pineapple Clubwich).
Photo: E. Zipern

"I tutor at the elementary school. Joey tutors at the high school there. Right now I have two six grade girls and I'm just teaching them reading and math and self-esteem. One of the girls I tutor I've learned more from than a lot of people, which is really neat. So she can teach me and I can teach her and that works nicely. A lot of respect that way. I love working with the children. I mean, that's the best part of living here, I think."

In Carbondale, Illinois, the bagel business has a long tradition. The city's streets are home to bagels, and lots of them. There, Rich runs a bagel cart for the bagel lover in everyone. Bagel fanatics can choose from nine different toppings ranging from cream cheese to sunflower seeds, onions, raisins, cucumbers, apples, cinnamon, butter and bacon bits. With so many topping choices, Rich figures there are a multitude of different combinations.

"With the nine ingredients I use in Carbondale, there's 362,800 combinations, but with the eleven I'm using here, it's like 42 billion combinations," Rich says while flipping bagels in the parking lot of the Deer Creek Music Center. "I mean, it's an estimate. I don't know the exact number, but it's obscene." (Actually, Rich thinks it's 39,916,800.)

Bagel carts are a long-standing practice in Carbondale, and there is stiff competition for them. The word is: when in Carbondale, get a bagel. "You usually don't see it on the street in any other town, so when people come back to Carbondale, they're like, 'Oooh, bagels!' " says Rich.

"It works out pretty good," he explains. "There used to be a bar entry age of eighteen, but they raised it to twenty-one now, so it has really hurt my business. But it's fun, it's like my social life when I'm in school, it's cool. I hang out on the scene, sell bagels just like this, goof around with people and stuff. And it's good food, you can treat people right for two bucks, make 'em really fat."

For a year, Rich's stand, dubbed "Fish's Bagel Cart," has been on U.S. Route 51 on "The Strip" in Carbondale. The road passes through three states, and it keeps him busy. When he's not in Carbondale, Rich and his girlfriend, Bridget, like

Bridget and Rich (THE ELEVEN Layer Bagel).
Photo: Mark Dabelstein

to bring the cart to Dead shows in Sarah Jane, their '71 white Volkswagen bus.

"It's a nice way to fund seeing the country," says Bridget. "We did all the West Coast tour. We get to see a lot of cool places. I think it's one of the best shopping malls in the world that brings in a lot of different types of people, and the food is different."

"The bagels are a good place to get tickets," Rich adds. "When we don't have them and we have the bagel cart, we always get tickets. I think you just talk to people more. People want to give tickets to people who are having a good time, making food, doing stuff."

THE ELEVEN Layer Bagel
Serves a bunch

Rich's Dead show motto: ``Come for the music, stay for the food.''

BAGELS
Onion
Poppy
Blueberry
Plain

LAYER TOPPINGS
Hummus
Cream cheese
Sunflower seeds
Sprouts
Spanish or white onions, diced
Raisins
Cucumbers, sliced
Apples, sliced
Cinnamon
Butter
Soy (imitation) bacon bits

• Put everything together, spread on a bagel and eat. A few tips from Rich.

ON HUMMUS. . .
"The recipe changes. We do it really scientifically. We measure it down to the microgram," he jokes. "No, I grab handfuls of beans and then I add tahini in a blender with a lot of lemon juice, onions, hot peppers, garlic, black pepper. Blend it up for a while really good. But making hummus on the road is a drag. You need a blender."

ON COMBINATIONS. . .
"I don't think that cinnamon and sprouts and hummus go together," says Rich (he has seen really weird combinations). But he does recommend the following: try apple, cinnamon, raisin and cream cheese. Also try cucumber, onion, sprouts and hummus.
"For the hobbled tour head, a bagel with everything is about four inches tall and will Phil you up for a long time."

As the occasional dog wanders over to check out the cheesy aroma arising from his hot, grilled cheese sandwich laden stove, Don flips the forever faithful parking lot staple. Every once in a while he looks up from spreading fresh herb blended margarine onto thick slices of twelve grain bread. He gauges the amount of sandwiches he needs to make by the number of customers waiting in front of his steaming stove. At this particular moment, Don's friend stands in front, anxious to get a sandwich and go inside to see the show.

"Hey, buddy, can you kick me one of those, I'm starving!" his friend says. Don takes one of the cheesy treats off the grill and hands over the sandwich in a paper towel as his friend bows in appreciation. "Thank you, my chef," says his friend as he turns to leave. Over the gathering of people surrounding him, Don calls out to him, "Say hi to the fat guy (a.k.a. Jerry Garcia) for me!"

It is December 19, the last show of the Dead's winter tour, and for four days, fans from all over Southern California have made it down the 110 Freeway toward the Los Angeles Sports Arena. It's the final show of 1994 and Don still doesn't have a ticket for tonight's show, but he remains content. In the last few hours he has successfully rounded up a number of Deadheads going east to share traveling expenses. The goal is to make it back to his parents' house in Michigan in time for Christmas. What will take him there is his baby, Rosie, a white 1966 Ford "Super Van," a vehicle that sometimes serves as his home and always as his traveling companion.

"It's a classic bus, a cool ride. A lot of people have cruised through the years in buses just like it.

Tall Don's Galactic Grilled Cheese Sandwich
Serves 1

Fresh chopped basil, to taste
Fresh chopped oregano, to taste
Garlic (Don uses granulated garlic, but you can use fresh or powdered)
Butter, margarine or vegetable oil (Don uses margarine because butter burns on his portable stove. At home use any of the above.)
2 slices of 12 grain bread or any good quality bread
4 or 5 slices real Wisconsin cheddar cheese

• To taste, mix the basil, oregano and garlic with the butter, margarine or vegetable oil. Spread the mixture on both sides of the bread, place a few slices of cheddar cheese in between, and close the sandwich.
• In a pan, heat the sandwich with a little butter, margarine or oil until the cheese becomes gooey and the outside is lightly brown.

It's a famous one," explains Don. "I don't want to get involved in the commercialism of buying new cars. I have one vehicle and it's going to last me my whole life. I know it, I'm just going to do it. I'm going to rebuild it too. It's going to transmute into something different twenty years from now I'm sure, but I'm committed to it. In my heart, I know it's what I want to do."

To support himself on the Lot and pay for tickets, Don usually sells Galactic Grilled Cheese, a traditional tour sandwich with a twist: basil, oregano and garlic. Don vends sandwiches to pay for all his touring needs, but mostly sells them because he doesn't feel comfortable in the Lot unless he is working.

"I like the Lot because it's the most intense love, the intense real family, real people experiencing reality, head-on. Facing life. We all love each other," he explains. "It's a different kind of love. It's people being conscious about trying to make a difference in the world and put this energy back into their lives. And they do something with it. It's being kind to yourself. That's so important. It starts there, then you go from there, and maybe eventually, the cup will spill over. Put a little energy back into it."

Don (Tall Don's Galactic Grilled Cheese).
Photo: E. Zipern

Don faithfully follows the Dead, mostly traveling in Rosie, because the band, the scene and the people are part of his life. "It's the soundtrack to my life," he remarks proudly. Don's first show was at Alpine Valley, Wisconsin, in 1988. The experience appealed to him instantly and he has been touring ever since.

"They're the most diverse band out there," proclaims Don. "This band represents almost every style of music. There's world beat, there's jazz, there's blues, there's rock 'n' roll, there's classical. It's just all there. It's a musical experience. And dancing to it is transformative, it's healing. That's what a lot of these people are doing here. Together we create this huge vibe, this healing vibe. We put it out and it's positive energy, you know? And then people take that energy back to their individual communities to actualize the healing.

"So much of my life has happened because the band is doing their thing and they let me do my thing, and together, good stuff happens. The shows that I've had, the way I've felt in the shows, I've never experienced anything like it in my life. There is no comparison. All I know is that I like to dance and I like to feel the positive energy of the people that are here.

"The only regret I've had in my life is that I didn't discover the Grateful Dead earlier. This is my home, man. My place. I'm a Deadhead. The only way I won't be here is if they put me in jail."

If you were one of the lucky souls to have chanced upon Scott Landis's sandwich setup before or after a Dead show in the last ten years, you were probably treated to his culinary labor of love. Before each show, Scott spent hours making Dead Bread, a sunflower-walnut wheat bread that became the base for his infamous creation. . . the Cozmicados Sandwich. On the warm, freshly baked bread he would spread brown mustard, alfalfa sprouts, slices of avocado and Monterey Jack cheese. He especially loves to pile on lots of avocado.

"When I lived in Michigan, I never had a ripe avocado," contends Scott. "I just thought that with avocados, when you got them ripe, they're really amazing and a good thing for vegetarians. If I was making a sandwich for me, this is what I would want. And I felt like if I'm going to come to the show, it's going to be a together scene, and it's going to be fresh. And for people that are veggie, they love that kind of thing, they like that big, hearty, hass avocado.

"After doing it for a while, I got kinda bummed with all the beer sales in the Lot, so I would sidle up to the schmaltziest, probably weren't-even-going-into-the-show types that I could find, and then I would talk to their crowd because they always had a line if they were selling Budweisers or whatever. I tried to say, 'Okay, you're going to be here a long day, it's hot out, you should get something in your stomach.' I felt like it was something I was into, but also on some level, that we're as responsible for the scene as the Dead are. I'm not knocking people when they're young, because I've done goofy things when I was a kid, too, but it seems like you get a lot of high school kids that show up and hang all day drinking beer.

"It seemed for me, the alcohol was getting to be a big problem, especially with people who were selling shots of tequila. I don't mind drinking a beer, but I just know there was a lot of

Scott (Cozmicados and Dead Bread). Photo: E. Zipern

people who don't go in at all and just get blasted and they're the ones that end up trying to break the doors down to get in. Just because the Dead is kind of a neat environment for all us Heads to assert our freedom, that doesn't mean it's anarchy." He laughs. "And if you're into that, you're probably going to deal with the cops, because you're blowing it on some level.

"There would be this announcement from Phil that they'd always say, no vending, no camping and that whole rap, and not that that affected most of us, but I felt like that some of the parking lot scenes really got to be ugly. And if I was potentially part of the problem, maybe I should raise consciousness along the way."

While in college, two years before he moved to California, Scott saw his first show. Back

Cozmicados and Dead Bread
Makes 2 pan-size loaves, about 5 1/2 x 9 1/4 inches

DEAD BREAD
"Making this bread is kind of a long process," says Scott. "I usually listen to the Dead while baking as a motivator. This is a whole wheat bread with a couple of different kinds of nuts, sunflower seeds and walnuts."

3 cups warm water
1 Tb. yeast (1 package)
1/4 to 1/2 cup honey
3/4 cup dry powdered milk

2 cups whole wheat flour
2 1/2 cups unbleached white flour (with more of both flours to be added after the first rising)

• Dissolve the yeast in warm water. Then, combine the above ingredients and mix well. Let rise in a large bowl until it doubles (which will depend on weather and humidity, but probably will take 45 minutes to an hour). On this first rising, you don't have to punch it down. It will foam up in the bowl and takes about 4 hours at the longest. "If it's cool weather, it can take a long time," says Scott. "Done in the winter, it's been an all-day affair!"
• After it rises, add:
    1 1/4 Tbs. salt
    1/4 to 1/2 cup oil or butter
    3 cups whole wheat flour
    1 1/2 cups of white flour
    1/4 cup walnut pieces (these nuts are optional. . . feel free to cook without them)
    1/4 cup sunflower seeds

• At this stage, Scott says it's like a sponge, a "big frothy thing. . . . The sweetener and the wheat and the flour are doing their thing. When you add the salt, that slows the rising part. Salt inhibits the yeast. With this and extra flour, you can knead it on a board. But before that it's kind of wet."
• Put it out on a board. Have 1 to 2 cups flour ready so the dough doesn't stick when kneading. Knead until smooth. Watch for it to double in size.
• Let rise twice for about 35-50 minutes each, punching it down each time.
• Cut into 2 pieces, shape and put into the pans. Let rise again for 15 minutes in the pans. Put the loaves into a 350° preheated oven. Baking time takes about an hour and the top should be brown when done.

COZMICADOS SANDWICH—THE PIÈCE DE RÉSISTANCE:
• Slice! Take two slices, and add:
    Brown mustard
    1/2 an avocado per sandwich, sliced
    Alfalfa sprouts, to taste
    Monterey Jack with jalapeno pepper pieces, sliced
• Arrange how you like and enjoy!

then, he had to drive over three hundred miles just to see the band, but that didn't matter. When he got his first taste of the Dead and the scene that surrounded them, he wanted more.

"At one point in my life, I thought the Grateful Dead was a country rock band, I was putting them in there with Skynard and Marshall Tucker," he explains. "July first of 1984 was my first show. I went, came home and said, 'We can blow off class and see two more this weekend!' We ended up going to Alpine right after the first shows we had seen.

"The crowd scene is a whole rush. I'm not into spending every weekend with crowds, but definitely think a good half or whole of the experience for me is checking out the glee of the first-time dosed-out person or just checking out the cars rolling in with the whole paint jobs, the parking lot and how the competing tape decks are going. And when I'm in that group, in the audience, and I'm just seeing people getting down and going nuts, that's good.

"I've read a bunch of press about the Dead, and all these different peoples' views of what they're about, and yeah, maybe it is just a tip of the hat to the old sixties Woodstock generation trip, but it's influenced by a lot other stuff too. It just seems like they stand for a lot of freedom."

In the square Lot across from the Seattle Memorial Stadium, Chris, Jimmy, Jason and Amanda, the proprietors of the Last Supper Kitchen, have set up a table behind their '66 yellow-white Shasta Camper. The round tow-along is hooked up to Jason and Amanda's van recently restored for the trip by Chris. He added a fridge, freezer, flat grill, deep fryer and an oven range. This and a picture of the Last Supper gave the four their start on tour together.

"We've done tours and we've done little things here and there, but this time we really decided to get our shit together," explains Chris. "We decided if we make money then we're going to shoot for land or whatever comes about is plenty. Every tour starts with a different reason. Different times of your life, different things will come around. I try not to plan too much. It usually ends up happening, but I try not to plan."

The group calls themselves the Last Supper Kitchen in recognition of the Last Supper poster that Jimmy acquired before he left Chicago.

"Jimmy told me that he was

Amanda, Jimmy, Jason, Chris (The Last Supper Fava Bean Sandwich and Salad).
Photo: E. Zipern

thinking of bringing this picture of the Last Supper," remembers Chris. "He brought it and he put it up there and it seemed pretty funny. We didn't really have a name, we didn't think about one till someone asked us if that was our name and it's been that way ever since."

To get the picture, Jimmy spent three and a half weeks trying to convince the older Macedonian woman in a bar he frequents to lend him the depiction that hung on her wall. She finally obliged and he brought it with him. Four days later, while driving through Mount Ida, Arkansas, on the way to tour, he had a car accident. When his car stopped rolling, Jimmy discovered the picture had come to rest in his lap, a questionable circumstance to many.

"I don't believe in that kind of conjecture anyway." Jimmy laughs. "It makes me think about it, but it gives me such a half-assed smile. I don't believe in God, but someone could take that episode and extrapolate a whole new book of the New Testament. But I'm glad we have the picture, and I'm sorry I bent and broke it."

For the 1995 summer West and East Coast tours, they made some of their specialities: hummus, falafel, tabouli and fava bean sandwiches. The four put together a mean batch of fava bean salad.

The Last Supper Fava Bean Sandwich and Salad
Serves a lot!

5 20 oz. cans (or 6 15 oz. cans) fava beans
1 20 oz. can garbanzo beans
4 bunches green onions, chopped
1/2 bunch parsley, chopped
1/2 cup olive oil

1 1/2 cups lemon juice
2 cloves fresh garlic, minced (or 1 Tb. garlic powder)
1/4 tsp. pepper
3 tsps. salt
1 small white onion, chopped

OPTIONAL (to make sandwiches or to just add to the salad)
Feta cheese, crumbled, to taste
Tomatoes, diced, to taste
4 or 5 pitas

• Mix ingredients and serve cold as salad or in a pita with feta and tomatoes.

Chris and Jason are familiar with Mediterranean food from cooking at Chris's family's restaurant, Papouli's Fine Mediterranean Foods, in Macon, Georgia. Over the years, they have been able to introduce Mediterranean food to the South, a difficult find in Georgia.

"It's in the middle of Georgia, there's nothing in Georgia, so we've been educating these people who know absolutely nothing about this food," explains Chris. "The majority of people who come in there, a lot of the time it's the first time they've heard of it, so you get to see the full effect.

"I've been cooking as far as I can remember. It's what I do, it's an art, it's fun. I love doing it out here, it's too good to be true. I like to see people eating it. I like to hear their compliments, makes you feel good. I guess being raised in it, I've been taught to aim for that look on a person's face when they take a bite.

On the morning of the first Dead show at The Omni in Atlanta, Donna spent hours cutting cabbage and cucumbers, mincing garlic and creating a delectable tahini dressing with fresh squeezed lemon. Once the vegetables were cut, she carefully stuffed them into pitas and then placed each sandwich inside of her square wicker basket to take to the Shakedown and sell.

As a vegetarian for four years and recently taking the plunge into veganism (no animal products at all) two years ago, Donna wanted to create a sandwich that would provide fresh vegetables for people to eat in the parking lot. Working in a health food store in Princeton, New Jersey, and on an organic farm has taught her about sustainable agriculture, growing organic vegetables and the food choices we all make, especially when eating on the road.

"Being vegan, you have to be creative, it just opens your world up to different things, to connecting food with some higher spirituality," says Donna. "It's important for me to be able to provide people with something that's completely animal free, nutritious and decadent. It's really a simple food that can be made quickly and a good road food to have because you can always score fresh vegetables.

"I just think it's important to be eating well, especially when you're out on the road," she continues. "Eating vegan on the road is tough, so you make the extra effort to find good health stores. It's also very important for me to make an effort to see these kinds of stores. In visiting different locations and seeing what other people are doing around the country, it spiritually gives me a lot of hope that people are moving away from a commercial diet and the four food groups which have been forced down our throats since we were five years old. It gives me hope that people are going to wake up and see that mainstream medicine and a national food chain isn't really feeding you.

"I'd rather support people on a local level. Support a local community, support a small shop owner, instead of supporting a national food chain where I don't know where they're sending my money. I'd rather give money back to a small community that is doing positive things because co-ops do more than just sell food. The co-op in Atlanta has different cooking classes, they have recycling programs and organic farming programs. Those places to me are more than grocery stores, they're sources of education. You can go and look on a bulletin board at a health food store and it opens up different realms of all sorts of things."

Going to shows, visiting co-ops and traveling around the country have introduced Donna to life outside of the mainstream.

"I think touring kind of opened me up to a different realm of

Donna (Organic Vegetable Pita).
Photo: E. Zipern

94

where I am in my own life," she explains. "When I first went to shows years ago, I was like, 'Wow, this is very different,' and it was a little scary to me in a sense, because it was different from the way that I was living and grew up. In turn that kind of snowballed and it brought me into a realm of looking at the world in different ways through talking to people and being educated and trying things, different food, on tour. In addition to the music, there's a lot of education that goes on in the Lot and you can zone into whichever part of that experience you want to, whether it's drugs or it's food or the people.

"It's a great way for people to be introduced to an alternative way of living. Use it as a mind and spiritual expansion, meeting and grooving with people, enjoying yourself and getting so high from dancing and listening to the music. It brings certain special people to that. The band has brought people together and introduced them to something different."

Organic Vegetable Pita with Tahini Dressing
Makes 2 sandwiches

This is a great recipe that keeps well on road trips or on tour. But keep in mind, the pita you use can make or break this sandwich. Donna says it is vital to find a good Lebanese or Middle Eastern bakery that makes fantastic pitas, so look hard. Use all organic vegetables! Make the sandwiches as fat as you want.

TAHINI DRESSING

1 Tb. fresh lemon
1/2 cup tahini
Lots of garlic, minced
1 Tb. vinegar (to preserve)
Add water to adjust consistency. If using as a dressing, add more water

PITA

2 pitas, cut in half to stuff or use whole
Red cabbage, shredded
Tomatoes, diced
Sunflower seeds
Carrots, shredded
Cucumbers, sliced thin

• Once the dressing is made, it is very easy to keep in the fridge as a spread. Tahini will keep for a while, especially with the vinegar and lemon as a preservative. Use it as a spread for sandwiches, in a salad, or whatever.

• Spread the tahini inside or on top of the pita. Cut the vegetables and stuff them into the pita.

Pasta

The last night of the winter Dead shows in L.A. is almost over, and mark one for the Angel City. Los Angeles has once again just about made it through four days of the Grateful Dead and their legions of passionate disciples trudging through the city clad in tie-dye, flower patterned dresses and hemp clothing.

As the sun slowly recedes behind a line of school buses in the Los Angeles Sports Arena parking lot, Deena and Arron sit at the back of Deena's mustard yellow Volkswagen Vanagon. Occasionally, they pick themselves up and glide over to their portable stove to stir the dish they created the night before—Thai fried noodles with tofu and vegetables.

"The shows catch up with me every now and then," proclaims Arron. "I don't chase Jerry. Though, sometimes I think he's following me." He chuckles, fixing the gas under the propane stove and then stirring more. "Hot Thai Noodles," he automatically yells out, sprinkling a dash of cayenne into the saute pan from time to time.

Eating, buying and then providing organic food is important to Deena and Arron. When they cook at shows, they sometimes have problems finding organic ingredients in bulk. "We had to go to three different health food stores to get the ingredients," laments Arron. "But it was definitely worth it. We've gotten a lot of good compliments out here. People were thanking us for bringing it.

"Eating organic promotes life on the planet for the soil, the water and every other part of the web of life," says Arron.

"And the ecosystem," adds Deena. "I feel healthier," she says. "Just more alive.

Deena and Aaron's Thai Fried Noodles. Photo: E. Zipern

Kind Vegan Organic Thai Fried Noodles with Tofu and Veggies
Serves 4

1 pound organic vegetable or soybean pasta

2 or 3 Tbs. olive oil

6 shakes cumin seed

1/2 cup tofu, sliced

3 Tbs. Thai Peanut Sauce. This can be store-bought or your own recipe. See page 78 for a recipe.

3 Tbs. tamari, or more to taste

1/2 cup each, cauliflower, carrots, onions, cabbage, sliced (or any other veggies you have around, in the same measurements)

1/4 cup minced cilantro

Cayenne to taste

• Boil the noodles, drain and let cool. Add oil and 6 shakes of cumin seed into a pan. Then, take two big handfuls of the pasta and saute over medium heat. Add the tofu, Thai Peanut Sauce, tamari and continue to stir-fry.

• Stir in the vegetables and cilantro by eye and continue to saute until everything is evenly coated and flavored and the veggies look "a little saucy," says Arron. To taste, sprinkle a pinch of cayenne into the mix. Stir and eat!

"Supporting organic is the best way we can give back to the earth," she continues. "Chemicals have gotten into our soil, our creeks, rivers and oceans, damaging all plant life, animals and us. Our air is polluted and our ozone, our breath of life, is crumbling. We need to stop our greed, get away from big business and live simply."

As crowds swarm in front of the Memphis Pyramid looking for a ticket to go inside, the late afternoon sun reflects a bright white light off the shiny triangular structure. In this light, Melissa, her father, Kendall, and his girlfriend, Pat, cook up pasta salad, hummus, lemonade and red beans and rice.

It is Melissa's 1995 spring break from high school and the three are on vacation together. They have opted to spend their time working, relaxing and hanging out at the Dead shows in Atlanta and Memphis. Melissa's school vacations are concentrated time that she and her dad have to be together, and sometimes they choose to spend it at shows.

Melissa, Kendall and Pat (Pat's Pasta Salad). Photo: E. Zipern

"We did Buckeye, two Chicago's, three Deer Creek's and three D.C.'s, so we did nine shows together, the East Coast basically," says Melissa. "All my friends know my dad and know that we go on tour together. He's not like a normal parent.

"My friends think it's really exciting," she continues. "It didn't bother me in the least that I was leaving town the day spring break began and I wasn't going to be back until school started. I didn't think for one minute, 'Oh, m'god, all my friends are having so much fun without me,' because not many people have experiences like this at my age. They have to wait until they're older and they're out of college, or they have to run away to do it.

"I really like the energy of the crowd here. Usually it's really positive and everybody has the same energy and feeling. I also like the acceptance that everyone has for everybody else. It's a feeling of unity, everybody is so giving."

Kendall, Pat and Melissa found that going to Dead shows gives them a perspective on their own lives. For Pat, observing the scene is an opportunity to learn. Graduating from the University of Louisville as a psychology major last June, she sometimes tries to relate her parking lot experiences to what she has learned in school.

"I've said this to other people," she contends. "You can gain more life experiences in three weeks with this tour if you're really perceptive and you really watch, than in four years at college. Psychologically you immediately see how you are drawn to those who are most like you, both economically and socially. You have the same reasons for being there, whether it's because you're a Deadhead, you're a follower of the Grateful Dead and you embrace that, whether you're a vendor, whatever. There's an adrenaline rush to the Lot experience, and that's fascinating when it all starts raging.

"I don't know if it is so much adrenaline, or the exhilaration you get because it's a little concentrated slice of life. The Lot is like a little ecosystem, and there's an energy about it that

Pat's Pasta Salad
Serves 6

1 pound tricolored rotini or spirals, cooked
1 medium yellow squash or zucchini, finely diced
1 medium zucchini, finely diced (if you're in the mood, add 2 zucchinis)
1 bunch broccoli, finely diced
3 large tomatoes, finely diced
1 bunch scallions (greens included), chopped fine
1 green pepper, finely diced
1/2 tsp. crushed red pepper
1/2 cup olive oil
1 Tb. oregano
1 Tb. basil (fresh is always nice too)
Black pepper and salt to taste
Balsamic Vinegar (optional)
Parmesan, sprinkled on top (optional)

• Cook the pasta according to package directions, drain, then set aside to cool.
• While the pasta is cooking, cut the vegetables. Pat says the key to making great pasta salad is to finely dice all the vegetables (very true).
• Once the pasta has cooled, add the vegetables, oil and spices. A little balsamic vinegar to taste is wonderful!
• Mix well, chill and serve. Parmesan cheese sprinkled on top can also be a nice touch if you eat dairy.

you get caught up in. Maybe that's a good way to describe this feeling. Maybe it really does have something to do with a collective energy and a collective sense of peace and harmony."

"The thing for us, both being parents, we had this thing tattooed on our heads that said 'Parents' and so the wayward kids in the Lot seem to find us," adds Kendall. "Especially Pat, she had two in Chicago that were just classic."

"We were safe havens," Pat continues. "We were safe havens because we were approachable and because we are not that hardcore looking. The general public who came down to see what was going on would first accustom themselves to the Lot by coming up and talking to us in order to feel more comfortable with their own surroundings. We found that some of the kids who had gotten themselves in too deep and maybe were a little more lost would have a tendency to come to us for help first, not for a handout. They would need reassurance or just a pat on the back, saying, 'You're okay, you'll be fine.'"

Viewing it from an older perspective, Pat and Kendall have been able to observe the problematic interactions between the communities surrounding venues, Deadheads and the police.

"From the beginning, I started seeing how the local communities and the law enforcement have been playing psychological head games in order to control the masses, in order to control the crowd," maintains Pat. "They do this to make a point. To panic the crowd, they randomly hit these kids. They just make examples of them. I mean, there must be people who do studies of this. How to control this beast? Little by little, they're doing it. They're taking it away from the inner cities and they're containing it on these little farms, these little Lots, and these little campgrounds. And it is going to be contained. Within the next few years, I think you won't be seeing stuff like this. It will always continue, but in an altered state."

Standing over his pot with a large ladle in hand, Jim stirs his creamy white, black pepper-speckled sauce as streams of people flow by him. The aroma from the homemade Alfredo sauce infuses the area, prompting many to linger at the front of his table and wait for the next batch to be ready.

"There's a whole group of guys standing over there," comments Jim, pointing across his spot on the Shakedown. "I think they've really got the munchies. One of the guys came over, got a plate and liked it so much that his buddies just started flowing over. Before I knew it, I had five guys in front of my table coming back for seconds and thirds. When people enjoy my food, it is the biggest compliment. It's a rush and an affirmation. It's a great satisfaction to be providing a wonderful thing for people. Helping them enjoy their show makes mine even better. What more could you want?

"In the past I've sold tie-dyes," he remarks, motioning to the bright, tie-dyed T-shirt he wears. "But this year I didn't have time to make them. I love to cook and I wouldn't feel right being at a show if I wasn't selling something on Shakedown."

Jim (Phatt-Fabulous Fettuccine Alfredo). Photo: Mark Dabelstein

Jim is cooking like mad, boiling pasta and mixing his savory Alfredo sauce at New Jersey's Giants Stadium, his first venue of the summer tour. This is the vacation that Jim has worked for. He is more than halfway through an eight-month break he set aside for himself to rest, go on

Jim's Phatt Fabulous Fettuccine Alfredo
Serves 4

"I just love to cook at home, it's a way for me to relax from a busy day, sort of my escape from reality," says Jim. "I've been cooking for three years and this sauce is just one of many, many, versions. Every time it comes out differently. I know where I'm going with it, but as I go along I sort of adapt it by how it looks and how I'm feeling. I started with a basic white sauce and expanded from that."

2 Tbs. extra virgin olive oil (can be substituted with fat-free Italian dressing)

1/2 onion, diced

10 to 12 cloves garlic, minced fine and to taste (as always)

2 Tbs. flour

2 cups skim or whole milk. Whole is creamier, but skim is healthier

1/4 cup white or Marsala wine

Black pepper, to taste

Oregano, to taste

Basil, to taste

Cayenne and/or white pepper, if you like it spicy

White granulated sugar, to taste (and to sweeten things up)

1/4 cup each Parmesan and Romano cheeses, grated

1 pound fettuccine, bow tie or shell pasta (though Jim is privy to bow tie)

• Heat the olive oil in a skillet and add the diced onion. Cook until tender, then add the minced garlic. (This will keep the garlic from burning while the onions cook.)

• Add 2 Tbs. flour and let it soak up the oil. Then add the milk. Jim says if you like a thicker sauce, add more flour. If it is too thick, you can always thin with more milk or wine.

• If you like wine, try adding a 1/4 cup of it when you add the milk. "Try a nice white wine," says Jim. "If you like the rich Italian flavor a bit more, go with a little Marsala wine. It will turn the sauce a brownish color, but it will add a wonderful complexity to the flavor. I probably overcook with the flavors, but I love it, so I just can't help but throw it all in."

• Add the spices to taste. Jim says this is not a traditional Alfredo sauce, but more of a creamy Italian sauce, so use what you like. Let simmer so the herbs can hydrate and release the oil from their leaves. A touch of sugar may be added to sweeten the sauce.

• At this point, be creative and add anything else you like into the dish. Jim suggests adding red pepper, chicken or Italian sausage, all of which will "add a variety of flavor."

• Toward the end of cooking, add the grated Parmesan and Romano cheeses at a low heat to melt. Don't bring the sauce to a boil or the cheese and the milk could curdle.

• Before the sauce is done cooking, cook the pasta. Pour the sauce over the pasta, put your favorite show into the tape deck, and enjoy!

Dead tour and then travel to Alaska and Hawaii to backpack and scuba dive. After graduating from the University of Michigan in December of 1994 and before beginning medical school at Harvard in September of 1995, Jim needs to take time for himself.

"I had to be on tour. I'm going to be a slave to the books again come fall," remarks Jim. "In med school I'm not going to have the ability to say, 'Hey, I'm taking a couple of weeks off and following the Dead.' This summer, I have the opportunity. I've worked long and hard for my dreams of going to medical school, but this also has always been a dream of mine; to follow the Dead for more than a short run of shows, to go on summer tour.

"I seriously thought about taking off a year after high school to follow the Dead because it's something spontaneous and exciting. I can sell my crafts on Shakedown while being surrounded by amazing people who are all here for the magic. I can go and dance at the shows and listen to a Scarlet-Fire that burns my heart and ignites my spirit. It's another world sitting out here talking to people, working with them and providing this. I couldn't be happier.

"I think the magic of the shows is the freedom that's expressed. It's a sense of detachment from the world that's just wonderful. When you're in the Lot, people are just having a great time. They are from all over the country with different reasons for following the Dead and there is the artistry of so many people. We have shirts that are hand embroidered, we've got jewelry, we've got food. It's just a really great group of people. I love talking with the vendors before the show gets out, just sitting and hanging before the rush in the parking lot, talking about that night's show.

"The music is the common bond that brings us all together. I love the jams, the freedom in the music, and the feeling that you never know what's going to come next. I mean, when they're out there, they don't even know what they're going to play next. Every show is different. Sometimes it's jazzy, others bluesy. They can really rock or be very mellow. Listening to a show is a truly amazing experience. There's a lot of energy in the music. It's a wonderful outlet for me."

Tempeh and Pasta with Peanut Sauce
Serves 4 to 6

1 pound (or just a nice head) broccoli, cut in small florets and the stalks cut in circles

1 8 oz. package tempeh, sliced

Olive oil

At least 5 or 6 cloves of garlic, minced (though John recommends half a head)

1 pound long, flat, soba noodles

PEANUT SAUCE—these amounts should be mixed by eye. Aim for a creamy, peanuty sauce.

Sesame oil and/or olive oil

Organic peanut butter

Braag (see Glossary for info.)

Fresh garlic, minced

Sesame seeds

- Steam the broccoli. As it steams, cut the tempeh in slices about an inch wide. Fry the slices in olive oil until golden brown, then add the broccoli with a bunch of garlic and continue to saute. In a large pot, cook the pasta.
- To prepare the peanut sauce, heat olive or sesame oil in another skillet. Add the peanut butter and braag. Add garlic and stir.
- Prepare the pasta, then add the broccoli and tempeh. Serve the sauce over it all, or another option is to pour the sauce into the wok and combine with the pasta, then mix together. Sprinkle sesame seeds over everything.

On a Guatemalen blanket spread out in a corner of the Sam Boyd Stadium parking lot's hard, dusty desert floor, John sits with his legs crossed, trying to stay cool in the stifling Las Vegas heat. Above him, a blue plastic tarp stretches between a Volkswagen bus and a van to help block out the glaring sun as he tried to sell tape covers. This is one show where John would prefer not to cook. Usually, he makes tempeh with pasta and peanut sauce, but as always, summer shows in Las Vegas are an unbearably hot place to cook in.

For years, John has been a regular in the parking lot. Since graduating from college in 1992, he has made a point to catch every tour with the Dead. Going to his first in 1987, John has seen almost three hundred shows and in the last year missed only one.

"It came to me in '88," notes John. "That was the first show that I knew, they just played so beautifully. And that's the first time that I saw the magic. I knew it would lead to something farther and deeper. It was a scene, something I had never seen before, but something that I was looking for."

Living on the road during and between tour for years, John has discovered favorite places to visit that are now regular stops in his travels. During his journeys, he'll travel to national parks, vast hiking areas and vegetarian restaurants. These have been an important part of John's Grateful Dead experiences.

"Just from traveling with the Grateful Dead, I know all the spots all over the country," he explains. "All of these hot springs, cool hiking spots. I know where you can sleep and you won't be hassled, I know good vegetarian restaurants all over. And I like driving with cool, mellow people. Like people who, if we're only one hundred miles from this magnificent natural creation, will drive to it and check it out, because that's what you gotta do. You can't make it just Grateful Dead, you can't go from parking lot to parking lot.

"We're making our own neighborhood in every city we go to. Like whatever city we're in, we stay together, we're all doing the same thing. Like the song goes, 'Typical city involved in a typical daydream,' it just kinda melts into one. I mean sometimes, I forget where I am."

Inside the shows, spinning has become a doorway into a spirituality of sorts for him, one he hadn't encountered before.

"There is a lack of spirituality in America, I was born and raised Catholic and it seems like those people are more adamant about certain religious practices because they have to be. Music is not part of their ritual, and that's what Grateful Dead is. I think I heard Mickey or someone say, 'We leave room for people to create ritual,' and that's what it is. Music is super important.

"I saw so many people doing it (spinning)," he explains. "It actually started out as a way to make room for myself dancing. My friend and I used to go down to the seats and flail. I'd have bruised knees and stuff, but I didn't care. We were just flailing down there, and it just got too much so I had to go out in the hallways. We were out in the hallway and I started spinning and never stopped.

"The way I look at it, it's Sufism American style. It's deep, heavy trance dancing. It's like we're tapping into something. You're becoming part of what's around you. Every particle in the world, everything spins in a circle, everything is a circle. It's like consciousness seeking its greater design. The only thing more natural to me is breathing."

The scorching hot burners hold two large silver woks full of steaming noodles and sizzling vegetables. Every few minutes a voice from behind the woks yells "Shang-hiiiiiii Noooodles!" into the crowd.

Paul, sometimes known as the Dankster, other times as Tie-dye Paul, borrowed the Shanghai noodle recipe from his friend Jack. A basic chow mein dish, Paul modified it slightly for Grateful Dead tour, replacing the egg noodles with rice noodles and the oyster sauce with soy sauce.

"I sat around for a long time and figured out what wasn't being sold on tour that is vegetarian and has lots of veggies," says Paul. "Jack and I kind of came up with chow mein from his family recipe. But it's still in the early stages.

Paul (Shanghai Noodles). Photo: Mark Dabelstein

"The main thing is just to feed the family, friends and everyone some good food, then go in and see Jerry. It's so important, when you come out of the shows after dancing so hard, it works out a huge appetite. You're starving after a show. A big plate of noodles is what people need to ground them. It's kind of like medicine food, just the bulk of it. And we get a really positive reaction. It's a way to make some honest ticket money; we put a lot of labor into it."

The first show Paul remembers seeing was in 1984 at the Henry J. Kaiser Arena in Oakland, California. Five years later when the scene began to explode, Paul stopped touring so he could open a booth offering tie-dyes in San Francisco.

"Tour was getting a little tough in the late eighties," Paul explains. "A lot of my friends went to prison, everyone was getting arrested, Brent died. That was kind of a blow for me, I kinda got a little freaked out, I didn't want to go to prison. So I chilled out, I just wanted to get my own thing going on. It took me a little while to get back to tour, this last spring tour was my first tour since '89.

"I just got really comfortable hanging out in San Francisco selling my tie-dyes everyday. It was really flowing, I was able to do my art, people were buying it, they loved it, no hassle. It was real easy and fun but it was time to stop doing that for a while. I went on spring tour and got into ten out of fifteen shows and just absolutely fell in love with tour again. Everybody was still on tour and they saved me a spot, it was like, no worries when I came back. Everybody was really happy to see me and it was just great to be back in the scene again.

Shanghai Noodles
Serves 4 to 5

1 pound rice noodles
3 Tbs. peanut oil
1/2 cup sliced cabbage
1/2 cup sliced celery (about 1 stalk)
1/2 cup sliced carrots (about 1 medium carrot)

1/2 cup sliced bok choy
1/2 cup sliced green onions
2 to 3 tsps. roasted sesame seeds
3 tsps. sesame oil
2 Tbs. soy sauce
Hot sauce, to taste

• Blanch the noodles, drain and let sit. Heat the wok, then add the peanut oil until it smokes. Add the noodles, the vegetables (all are optional except the green onions), roasted sesame seeds, sesame oil and then soy sauce. Saute for 1 to 2 minutes on a high heat.
• Serve with hot sauce and fortune cookies.

"The Dead are the greatest rock and roll band in the world, the most psychedelic band there is, the hardest working band, the greatest touring band. They're just full of good, wholesome Grateful Dead family values." He smiles. "I believe the Grateful Dead is just one of the most positive things going on right now in this country. The way they pull us all together for some music for a few days and then have a week off where we go to the rivers, camping, we roam around a little bit, and then we come back together. It's a nice balance of music and getting totally loose with other stuff, like kids and family and hanging out with your friends. And then, just when you're ready again to get back together, there's another show and it's just so killer and it just keeps going. I love it, it's so sweet.

"When the band plays together and they're all onstage, something happens, it's magical. The combined energy of everyone being in the show together, it's hard to describe. I get this total warm feeling every time I get in a show and I get around everybody who is dancing and enjoying the music and the Dead are just wailing, they rule. It's positive and I just love it, everybody's loving it. That must keep people coming back. It's the unity and stuff that we get when we're in there and the togetherness that happens and the lyrics, the songs and everything. It's like they combine into our lives. It's totally cool."

By early morning, the word was out that the second show scheduled at the Deer Creek Music Center outside of Indianapolis had been canceled. For the first time in Grateful Dead history, a concert was called off for fear of trouble breaking out. The previous night had been intense. A riotous mass of concert goers tore down the Center's fence, presenting a dangerous situation for those inside, and ruining the Dead's chances of ever playing there again.

As a result, thousands were left wandering the Indianapolis area. Some drove on to the next scheduled shows in Chicago while others were stranded, unable to hook up with desperately needed rides. Impromptu Shakedowns began materializing in area campgrounds. There, Deadheads discussed what happened, hung around and figured out what to do next. Campground scenes soon began to take the form and feel of a Grateful Dead parking lot. Allie was at one such campground, situated ten miles from the arena and next to a reservoir that Deadheads played and swam in all day. She was one of many who began cooking to feed everyone.

Allie and Cedar (TVP with Pasta and Sauce). Photo: Mark Dabelstein

"When we came here last night, we just started chopping. I brought two grills, set up a little thing outside the van and started cooking," says Allie. "I don't have a lantern, so after this venue I'll get my lantern so I'll be able to see better. Usually I live with a lot of people even when I'm stationary, and I love being head chef. I've got a full-on kitchen, spices and all kinds of things. I like to cook for a lot of people and it's always just by smells and what looks good."

In the campground, Allie dished up TVP (Texturized Vegetable Protein) with pasta and sauce. Allie loved introducing the TVP to many who had never heard of or tasted it before.

"When I was cooking last night, my friend Sean asked what's in it. I told him the ingredients and said there is TVP in it, and he's like, 'What is that?' I guess he wasn't vegetarian but I said it's really good, it's textured vegetable protein. He thought that was really gross." She laughs. "I think that a lot of people would try it because they don't know what it is. Same with the sweet peanut sauce on the pancakes this morning. I kinda forced people to try it. They were like, 'Uh, no, I don't think so, I'll just have syrup.'"

TVP with Pasta and Sauce
Servings are up to you

TVP (Texturized Vegetable Protein) is made from soybeans. It comes in granules, flakes, chunks and in 1-to-2-inch-long slices. When cooked, TVP should be tender (especially the chunklets). To cook, rehydrate and then refrigerate.

Allie says to stuff as many veggies as you can into your sauce. Cut them any way you like. She cooks by the way it looks and smells. Explore by taste and smell.

Vegetable oil
Onions
Green pepper
Broccoli
Carrots
Cauliflower
2 cans crushed tomatoes
Cayenne
Cumin
Oregano
Basil
Rosemary
TVP chunks (Let it cook in. Makes the sauce chunkier)
Miso ("I add it to everything I can!" she says. "The culture is alive! Adds life to your life!")
Cooked pasta

• Prepare the TVP by pouring a little less than a cup of boiling water over a cup of TVP. Stir and let stand 5 or 10 minutes to rehydrate. Vegetable broth or stock can be substituted for water (see page 4 for Carla's Sumptuous Soup Stock recipe).
• In a skillet, saute the onions in vegetable oil. Then, add the rest of the vegetables according to hardness and your inspiration. Let cook, then throw in the cans of tomatoes, spices, the TVP and miso. Simmer and let the flavors meld for 1 to 2 hours.
• Serve over pasta.

110

For the last two years, Allie and her dog, Cedar, have lived in Allie's '78 Chevy conversion van. Allie likes being able to travel and live outside, on the road. Sometimes she'll stop to visit with friends, especially if it gets cold, but for the most part, she likes to keep moving so she makes her home inside the van.

"There is no rent, just gas. I can park anywhere and I don't have a desire to put down roots, yet, so I just keep on movin,'" Allie explains. "Sometimes I stop to work and just set up my little alarm clock. I light candles, my bed is all set up, make some tea, it's my home! I love going to hot springs, always having free hot water, a five-hour bath in the springs. That's luxury.

"And I love the shows. There's an intensity and overall good feeling that you can't find anywhere else. I love the music, the lyrics. . . Jerry. . . it lifts me up and I dance on air during the show. It just feels good. If I had the money, I would spend less time in the parking lot (or campground) working.

"The music and the fact that I haven't seen many shows and there isn't many left is keeping me going. When I get shut out, I'm like, 'Let's leave, this parking lot sucks, let's go to the woods.' Then there's one more show in the venue, so I stay and get in and then I go to the next one. It usually happens like that. I never plan to do the whole tour, sometimes it just happens. The music is good and because there's a lot of people that I know and this is where I'll find them, it's hard to leave so many of the people I love so much."

How Sweet It Is. . .

Sweet Treats
*Makes 3 dozen

* "Every time I make them, they come out different," says Erin. "Sometimes gooey, sometimes crunchy, sometimes like candy."

1/2 12 oz. bag semisweet chocolate chips (any kind of chip. Try carob, peanut butter, vanilla, whatever. . .)
1 tsp. margarine

1 15 oz. can sweetened condensed milk
1/2 cup peanut butter, sunflower seed butter, or tahini
1 small (about 12 oz.) bag shredded coconut

• Melt the chocolate chips and the margarine. Pour in the remaining ingredients, adding enough coconut until you obtain a consistency thick enough to place on a cookie sheet. Mix well. It will not be as firm as regular cookie batter, but it will be a big goop of yummy, sweet batter.
• Preheat oven to 375° and bake for 8 to 10 minutes on a cookie sheet.
• Erin suggests placing some of the uncooked batter between two graham crackers and letting it melt in the oven, over a stove or fire.

Depending on which Lot you were in at the Portland Meadows 1995 Dead show, vending was split between a paved parking lot and adjacent sidewalks, and the dusty back parking lot. Both Lots were busy all day and featured the usual wave of vending sounds bouncing through the air.

Kate, her boyfriend, Allen, and their dog, Alice, were in these Lots, vending Kate's homemade gingerbread. Surrounded by friends and Alice, who sometimes wandered off, Kate loved selling the dessert.

"I thought selling gingerbread was fun, it makes me happy, spreads my light in a harmless way, and I knew I was making something people would enjoy," says Kate. "I like when I don't have to yell out gingerbread at all. Except when I've had a couple of good beers, then I'm much more bold in my sales.

"People always ask if they are brownies, but there is no chocolate in them. They're dark because of the molasses. The best thing is when people come back after trying them at a different show and they give twenty dollars and don't want any change. . . just gingerbread!

Kate was introduced to the Grateful Dead in high school when she lived in England. It was in 1990 on the Dead's European tour that Kate saw her first show. In Brussels to play a high school field hockey match, she decided to bail on the game (consequently getting kicked off the team) to see the Dead. She supported the venture by designing, silk-screening and selling T-shirts, her first enterprise.

"I totally was into being part of it, instead of just a visitor, a spectator or somebody that takes it all in. I liked being active in it, that's what started it all off," explains Kate. "Then I went to college, and my whole freshman year was all about going to see the Grateful Dead, or seeing the Jerry Garcia Band. It was cool, progressively you evolved with it, you came to understand more, see your roles, how you could take it in, how it could make you feel, because you could manipulate it. All these experiences. I've sold dresses, I've sold food, I've done hair wraps. All these different perspectives until you finally sort of transcend all of that and the main experience, is like, 'I'm here with the Grateful Dead. . . nothing else matters.'

"I'm so glad I was around to experience that, even though it has only been six or seven years. But I feel like, I totally got it, it hit home, I don't know what I'd be without it, and I think that's all you need to take from it.

"I guess it strikes such a chord, it resonates in your soul, it touches every part of your inside, it's just pure sensation. You are just so alive, right and then and there. The chords Jerry plays totally speak to you, and you're alive, and people can see that in you. It's really easy to see who's alive and then the people who are preoccupied with whatever day's trash is in their head, and they're not at that space.

"Every time they played 'Eyes,' I can't tell you how high I was. You're soaring up high in a really personal, sacred space. No one can touch me when I'm that high and lost in the chords Jerry plays. I wait for those lullabies that resonate in my soul and let me soar. It's truly my bliss.

"A lot of people have made that their way of reaching their bliss for such a long time. It's been pretty easy to call the 1-800 line and figure out where the next shows are so you can go track down that bliss. It scares me now that it's not that easy for us. We've got to find other ways, and I don't know if there are any other releases that make me feel that high. It's sort of a challenge. We have to rise to the occasion. You can't really live without it now that you've had it. You can cherish it, but I don't want to put that in a box, I don't want it to go away, I want to find out how to keep it going and do something else."

Kate loves vending and contributing to the Lot experience. Seeing the way others have contributed to the scene over the years has shown her a simpler, less consumer driven way of life.

"I feel like that set off this whole vein in me that had never been opened up before, in that everything is handmade," she explains. "I'm making paper right now, I make soap, I sew. I think that without this Grateful Dead experience, I would never have thought it was wrong to eat Kraft macaroni and cheese, or I would have never thought that it was wrong to go buy Ivory Soap, or figured out that I could do it on my own. Now, whatever I see in the store, I know it's inferior to something that is coming from my soul, from my hands. It gives me the ability to make everything. I feel like I am surrounded by people my age who are so capable of doing everything, they can make drums, they can blow glass, they can make food, people that make every type of food, all these people are picking up these trades.

"It's really not the Brady Bunch anymore, it's not having a maid and eating hot dogs out of the package. It's doing it all yourself, it's not hard, it's so accessible to learn, and I think that's generated and kept up through the Grateful Dead Lot. It just feels better to blend those things into your life as much as you can, and what you can't do, you can't do. I don't think I would have had the confidence or the know-how or the ingenuity to do any of that, without the Grateful Dead."

Alice's Vegan Gingerbread
Makes 25 3-inch-high pieces

*You'll need a 15 3/4-by-11 1/4 pan to make this

DRY STUFF
1 1/2 Tbs. salt
5 Tbs. ground ginger powder
2 Tbs. baking soda
8 cups whole wheat organic pastry flour, sifted
Cardamom, nutmeg, cinnamon, to taste. Use whatever you feel

WET INGREDIENTS
1 cup extra virgin cold pressed light oil (canola)
1 cup soy margarine, butter or "flavored" butter
4 cups light molasses, unsulfured and organic. Kate says if you don't
    have 4 cups, don't stress. Any combination of brown sugar, brown
    rice syrup or sucannot can be added to make up the difference
3 1/2 cups hot water (dissolves the molasses)

• Sift and mix together the dry ingredients very well. Add the cardamom, ginger and cinnamon and make sure to mix them in well
among the other dry ingredients. Kate recommends mixing the dry
ingredients over and over again until you're too tired to do it anymore.
• Mix the dry and wet ingredients together. This will become the consistency of thick cake batter. Pour into a waxed pan.
• Bake at 350° for 45 minutes until it looks like a spongy cake. Let
cool, then cut.

Kate (Alice's Vegan Gingerbread).
Photo: E. Zipern

116

Ashley Alderman's recipe for Congo Bars, a sweet, chocolate chip dessert, is at least three lifetimes old. It has passed through three generations in her family and looks like it may keep going. When she was young she can remember being excited whenever her mom would make them. In recent years the recipe has been adapted by her mom, but is still loved in the Alderman family.

"You just have to say Congo Bars and everyone in my house salivates," exclaims Ashley. "When I was making them to take to Memphis, my dad was upset because I didn't save him any. Of course if I make anything and I don't save him some, he gets upset."

To her dad's dismay, Ashley brought the Congo Bars, as well as whole wheat banana bread and peanut butter cookies to the shows in Memphis where the sweets were spread further into the Dead family.

"I'm just speculating, but I think it has to do with the nuts and the brown sugar and chocolate all thrown in there, all mixed into one," she says. "Sort of how the Congo is."

The Memphis Pyramid shows were the second venue where Ashley has seen the Dead. Though she had always wanted to go, Ashley found herself working or going to school whenever the Dead came around. Reflecting on her first experiences, she began wondering what she had been missing all those years.

"I just haven't gotten a chance to go to shows," she comments. "I really thought about it and I can't believe I've missed out on this for so long. So many of my friends have been on tour, and I've always thought that that was so great. Lately I've been really wanting to do more adventurous things. I now have the opportunity to do it and the means to do it, so I'm going to try to do a lot more traveling.

"Come next May, my roommate and I are going to pack everything up, put it in storage and just travel around and be free for about a year. We're going to go wherever anything takes us. I feel like I've got the letters to say that I have the education, but life is what really educates you; you learn so much from meeting people."

Ashley grew up in Boone, North Carolina, where music has always been an integral part of her community. With her family, she went to clogging, bluegrass and square dances. These experiences have helped her to appreciate music and where many of the Grateful Dead's musical roots arise from.

"Where I live in North Carolina is very well known for its bluegrass music and all kinds of different music coming up through the wings," she explains. "I think that the Grateful Dead combine a lot of different types of music for their sound and I like that. I like their lyrics, too, they really say a lot to people, especially in this new way that we are starting to view the

117

world. It's old age actually. Just a lot of very spiritual things that they have to say. I think it has to do with community too. You see good community in their lyrics and within the whole culture that surrounds going to Grateful Dead shows. You meet so many neat people and hear so much great music.

"People come and although they don't realize that they are doing it, they study other people. It's a neat way to get into a subculture and feel like you belong. I think people feel it's okay to be an individual and to be your own person and that you're not going to be judged for being different. That's a lot of the draw too. People really appreciate individuality. It's as if everybody is an individual but at the same time there is oneness going on.

"I especially noticed it in Memphis. There's every walk of life, from eighty-year-olds to newborns, from every socio-economic background and everybody appreciates that. Nobody judges anybody else for who they are or where they are in life. That's important when we get all caught up in what society expects us to do and that whole system of being, but when you get to Dead shows, you forget all that. Everyone is sort of appreciating where everybody else is in life, nobody has to have a nine to five job, nobody has to make a lot of money and be all things to all people. That's what really struck me. I think we really lost a lot of community with the way we set up society now, the way the government has set us up to be, to bite and scratch for what we need, instead of working together for what we need."

Ashley and Kristi (Congo Bars). Photo: E. Zipern

118

Ashley has her undergraduate degree in sociology and in 1994, she received her master's in English which she now teaches at the college level. After extensive traveling, Ashley plans to join others in her area to begin seriously creating a sustainable community. Together they plan to buy land, build structures and gardens, and start an agriculturally based alternative school for children that would tentatively combine Waldorf and Montessori teaching methods.

"We're in the discussion stages right now. It's friends and others—a handful of us who are really dedicated to seeing it happen," she says. "It wouldn't be as if we were cut off from the rest of the world. We want to be able to invite people in to learn about what we're doing, and learn about sustainable development, about our school and holistic health. We're going to make ourselves be educators for other people who are interested in that. People are really starting to realize that we're on the wrong track and they're going to want a way to learn how to get back on whatever the right track is for them. I feel like we want to be that means for them to come together to learn about a different way of living rather than living in a high-rise. It's getting back to learning about what the earth has to offer us. . . in terms of her gifts and in terms of the whole spiritual base."

Congo Bars

Makes about 25 squares, depending on how they're cut
The ultimate in rich desserts!

1 5/8 sticks butter or margarine (almost 2 sticks), melted
1 pound box light brown sugar
3 eggs
1 tsp. vanilla
2 3/4 cups plain unbleached white flour

2 1/2 tsps. baking powder
1/2 tsp. salt
1 cup chopped nuts. Pecans, walnuts or any other mixture
1 small bag (about 12 oz.) semi-sweet chocolate bits or carob chips

• In a bowl, combine melted butter and the brown sugar. Let cool. Add the eggs one at a time and then the vanilla. Mix well.
• In another bowl, add the dry ingredients together, mix and then add to the liquid mixture. Mix everything thoroughly.
• Spread into a greased 10 x 15 inch pan.
• Bake at 350° for 20 to 30 minutes or until light brown (test with a toothpick or knife to check if it's done). Let cool and cut into small squares. Ashley thinks the bigger you cut them, the better. Enjoy with rice, soy, almond or regular milk.

In addition to the sounds of the Grateful Dead, vehicles in Dead show parking lots always have an assortment of music flowing from their radios. Music of Phish, jazz, Blues Traveler and reggae are common while walking past the tape decks and radios perched high upon Volkswagen buses.

Reggae has always especially appealed to Deadheads, in and out of the parking lot. Rastafarian doctrine has made a strong impact on an already spiritual community. The Rasta creed has reached far past its Jamaican birthplace and out into the world by one of its most popular messengers, Bob Marley. Marley's mystical, transitive chants about revolution, uprising and Jah have given the masses a peek into Rasta life. Marley's music lives on to familiarize others with the Rasta faith.

Rasta ideology believes in putting only pure and natural substances into the body. An Ital diet, a system of taking in only what is pure, excludes dairy, alcohol, refined sugars, salt, bleached or enriched white flours and some meat and fish. The idea is to give thanks for the gift of existence, giving thanks and praise to Jah, the Creator.

In recent years, the Dead community has embraced this lifestyle, and particularly the Ital diet. Now, traces of these ideas can be found throughout Dead lots.

Wendy and Natalie (Apple Spice Walnut Ital Baklava).
Photo: E. Zipern

In a far Shakedown aisle in the tiny parking lot across from the Seattle Memorial Stadium, Natalie and Wendy set up their kitchen. Their cooking is unique, the aim is to provide good Ital food in the parking lot.

Wendy slowly prepares organic stir-fry with marinated tofu and fresh greens over rice. Each plate is served with makeshift utensils; small, thin sticks the size of chopsticks that work surprisingly well. Along with the stir-fry, they made two desserts that are fairly time consuming and involved; sprouted manna and vegan baklava. Both Wendy and Natalie are deeply committed to eating organic, vegan, Ital food.

"Ital means natural," explains Wendy. "It's Jamaican, Creole. It means natural, from the earth. What comes out of the mother is Ital." She smiles thinking about it. "Because it is healthy body, healthy mind. Strong body, strong mind. You are what you eat. I like to cook with Jah creation, to cook with what Jah has provided, what the earth has provided.

Apple Spice Walnut Ital Baklava
Makes one 12-by-17 inch pan

*This takes about 3 hours to prepare.

4 organic apples	3/4 cup organic honey
Cinnamon, to taste	1/2 to 1 cup organic walnuts, chopped
Unrefined cane sugar, to taste	1/2 cup soy margarine, melted
3/4 cup organic sesame tahini	1 16 oz. package of phyllo dough

• Begin by preparing the apple butter which is simply a mixture of organic apples melted down with cinnamon and unrefined cane sugar. Take a few organic apples, core them, and with the skins on, chop them into small pieces. If your apples are not organic, Wendy and Natalie recommend peeling the skins before chopping.

• In a pan, combine the apples with a small amount of water. Cook down to a sauce and blend until smooth. Add cinnamon and cane sugar and let cool.

• Now prepare the tahini-nut mixture. In a bowl, combine the tahini, honey and chopped walnuts. In a sauce pan, lightly melt the soy margarine.

• Lay the phyllo dough out in a 12-by-17-inch pan and begin the process. Lay the tahini-nut mixture and apple butter onto the dough in layers, remembering to pat each layer down lightly. The idea is to create a few crispy pastry layers, then a few layers of the tahini mixture and apple butter.

• Lightly brush a layer of soy margarine onto the bottom of the pan. Then lay down 10 separate layers of dough, brushing each with a thin layer of soy margarine before the next layer is put down.

• On the 11th layer, lightly brush with soy margarine, then put a layer of apple butter, then another layer of dough, brush with soy margarine, then apple butter. Now add another layer of dough, brush with soy margarine, then tahini mixture, then dough, then apple butter, then dough, then the tahini mixture. Each layer you lay down, lightly brush soy margarine before adding anything else.

• Continue this in alternating layers, rotating the apple butter and tahini mixture. Save 4 dough layers for the end and lightly brush soy margarine on them with nothing else. Before baking, cut into squares.

• Bake at 350° for 20 minutes or until lightly golden. Once baked, pour honey or maple syrup (with cinnamon) over the baklava so it saturates.

"It's like, how can you have a clear mind if you don't have a clear body?" she continues. "Peace has to be in your head before you can carry it out with other people. It's a whole lifestyle, it's not just what you eat. It's how you carry your life. If you're positive, you're so much higher when you're eating. It's Rasta, it's being one with nature."

"To live Ital I've discovered through my philosophical studies of Eastern religion and of touching the source; that which is I, and we are all I," explains Natalie. "I started off vegetarian, then I was vegan and then I just became more and more conscious of exactly what is going into my body, because you can feel it. You become conscious of what is going into you and that energy and then what you're putting out. Then I became conscious of organics and only pure sources that come from mother earth. That's what ITALizes my body every day.

"Once you become aware of such a righteous consciousness, how can you not be kind to your body? Your body is a temple because Jah created your body for your mind, spirit and soul to live in. And so you want to preserve that, because in evolution, not everyone gets the opportunity to evolve into a human form."

Wendy and Natalie met in Boulder, Colorado, while living in a completely organic Ital household, meaning, no dairy, eggs, oils, alcohol, smoking, chemicals, shoes off inside and no drugs, but as they both point out, ganja isn't a drug. Ganja is the mother, it is sacred.

"It rises you to higher heights," explains Natalie. "It doesn't bring you down."

"Yes, I," Wendy answers Natalie as she speaks of the herb.

Shortly before the West Coast tour began, the two left Colorado to travel the country together.

"We work well together," observes Natalie. "When you're both conscious of the I, to combine that energy into a pair and to create the organics of the same source is creating channels for the energy to flow out into open space for everybody."

"It's a whole lifestyle, and when you lead the same lifestyle, it's very natural," says Wendy.

"Very pure," Natalie adds. "It's like simplicity, roots."

"To be on the Lot here, serving Itals is serving consciousness," maintains Natalie. "To talk to people, to educate people so they can learn about themselves and to take care of themselves. The Grateful Dead is a gathering of people, and to serve righteous Itals is to serve God because you're educating people on how to live and to survive for the self."

"I think it's important for this consciousness to spread out. Ital is vital. Eat well, you'll feel good," says Wendy. "It's a whole mind-body philosophy, it's a whole lifestyle, a whole energy. It's Rasta fari. Jah live."

The rust-colored Mars-like mountains behind the Sam Boyd Stadium in Las Vegas provide a stark backdrop for the deep, blue, searing sunlit sky. Reaching high up into the Las Vegas sun, the peaks cradle an early rising moon and the temperature, as always, is unbelievably hot.

Corrie Colbert and her sister, Kellie, walk along the parking lot's edge through mini-dust tornadoes that scatter microscopic dirt on everything and everyone. Wrapped in Corrie's hands rests a wide wicker basket filled with homemade hemp seed cookies. Each time she stops to sell a cookie, a crowd gathers. People seem to enjoy peering down into the basket at the batch of sweet, buttery treats, baked especially for the over 100 degree desert shows.

"Vegas was a hot one this year for sure, the cookies got a little soft, but hot weather is great, people seem more alive when it's warm," says Corrie. "I love the Vegas shows. The Sam Boyd Stadium with the mountains behind is beautiful. When it's really hot, everybody just strips down to almost nothing, but we have a good time."

Corrie ended up at her first show by accident. In 1992 she and a friend were driving through Las Vegas and decided to stop in the parking lot. Three years later, her life is filled with new experiences and opportunities, discovered by going to Grateful Dead shows.

"The Dead opened up such an outlet for me, I was introduced to so many new great lifestyles. Crafts, healthy cooking. . . hemp. It's like, you realize how creative you are. My first show I remember being so happy," she explains. "It's just amazing, it's a whole new world, brothers and sisters coming together, doing whatever they want to do at any time and being accepted for it. After that continual feeling of joy and love, you just want to keep going, just keep going further, further. The shows put everybody on the same plane, in the same place, having a good time. But it's all about music, and love, and everybody just comes together to be one, it's pretty amazing what music can do.

"That summer I discovered hemp with crafts and cooking. I just got into hemp that way, and there are so many great things you can do with it. I started cooking with the seeds and making jewel-

Corrie (Hemp Seed Cookies). Photo: Alec Bauer

Hemp Seed Cookies of Joy
Makes a bunch

*Add plenty of goodies to this recipe. Try coconut, nuts, fruit, etc.
*To roast the hemp seeds, spread them onto a cookie sheet and roast for 25 minutes or until brown and crunchy at 250°. Another option is to dry roast them in a skillet or wok. Either way, remember to wash thoroughly before cooking.

1 cup margarine, melted
1 1/2 cups brown sugar
1 tsp. vanilla
1 egg or an egg substitute
    equivalent to 1 egg
2 cups whole wheat flour
1/4 cup soy flour
1/4 cup oatmeal
1 tsp. baking soda

1 tsp. salt (optional)
1/4 cup roasted hemp seeds,
    ground (A coffee or grain
    grinder will work to grind
    them. Grind twice if needed.)
1/4 cup raisins
3/4 cup chocolate chips
1/4 cup whole hemp seeds,
    roasted

• Mix the margarine, sugar, vanilla and egg in a large bowl until creamy. In another bowl, mix the flours, oatmeal, baking soda, salt and ground hemp seeds. Gradually add the dry mixture to the bowl with wet ingredients. Mix well and add raisins, chocolate chips and whole hemp seeds.
• Drop the batter onto an ungreased cookie sheet and bake at 375° for about 9 minutes. Or, for cookie bars, spread the dough into a greased pan and bake at 375° for 20 minutes. Mmmm. . .

ry with the twine. Hemp is so good for you, that's the main thing, you just have to treat your body good.

"I started making the cookies because I didn't really know of any other way to eat the seeds. It started with your basic cookie recipe. I toasted the hemp seeds, started altering the recipe using soy flour and adding things that were good for you. They're a great thing to bake with, you can grind toasted seeds into a flour or use them whole. I've just been experimenting with them.

"So many people think that if they eat a hemp seed cookie, they're going to get high, because many have no idea that you can eat hemp products. If you want to get high, that's great, I mean, use the plant in as many ways as possible, but hemp seeds are so good for you. A lot of it is education. That's why I only charge a quarter a cookie for them. I don't make a lot of money, but that's not my purpose, it's like somehow you'll get there, the vibe will just carry you there."

The intensity of the sun around Portland Meadows took everyone by surprise. People were everywhere, walking around the Oregon venue in tie-dyes, patched cotton dresses and hemp shoes. Exposed to the bright sun, skin soon became a crisp, crimson while puppies hid under cars, trying to escape the heat.

The sun didn't let up until nightfall, and Shannon Keaveny's box full of sweet, gooey caramel dipped candy apples were melting. By late afternoon, the caramel surrounding the apples was mushy and sticking to the tinfoil, but still an incredibly yummy treat.

Shannon and her friends Wendy, Kate and Chris spent the previous day sticking popsicle sticks into apples, dipping them into a hot bath of caramel and then wrapping each in tinfoil and wax paper. The four enhanced the treats by writing lyrics, sayings, fortunes, quotes and one-liners on each popsicle stick; something for people to consider as they ate. They named the dessert Fortune Candy Apples.

"We took Dead lyrics and put them down and we also incorporated the apples into the lyrics with some of them," Shannon says. "We had three people working on them and we did one hundred and fifty sticks of just favorite quotes out of our life and little one-liners that we could think of. I'm an English major so I did a lot of poetry, quotes from poems that I like. We were psyched, we thought this was such an original idea because you go to a Dead show and there are sandwiches, beer, cold drinks and not much else."

Shannon lives and goes to school in Eugene, Oregon. Her first show was in 1989 in Minneapolis when she was seventeen. For the last three years she has sold food to help pay for the trips to see Dead shows.

"Every show that I've gone to for the last few years I've sold food, and the main reason is that Dead shows are expensive," she explains. "It's a really good time, but it's fun to walk out of the weekend and be even, not in the hole. I've made money before, but all I really want is to break even. I like to pay for my supplies and pay for my tickets. And it's fun, you feel more a part of the whole scene. You feel like you have a purpose rather than just standing or walking around.

Shannon (Fortune Candy Apples).
Photo: E. Zipern

"I love the music, I like the people, I like the scene, I always see people that I haven't seen in years. There's people here from all over the United States and the world. I've lived in all different places so there's people that I feel I'll never see again, but a lot of times I run into them here, it's neat."

Shannon thinks the Dead's attraction not only has to do with the music but also with the cohesiveness found within the Grateful Dead scene.

"There's a sense of community among people. People kind of let down, they share. Everyone is real mellow about things and not so caught up in the rat race," she observes. "There's something totally missing in our society and people find it here. People get caught up in the spirit of it and it's fun. There's a big karma feeling. You do something for someone else and it will come back to you. I think a lot of people are like that.

"There have been times when I've been in the parking lot at two o'clock in the morning and didn't have a ride, didn't have a blanket, and people were giving me blankets, trying to put me up for the night. It's a family feeling, people caring about each other."

Fortune Candy Apples
Makes 4 candy apples

16 caramels (or more. . .roughly 4 caramels per apple)
1/4 stick of butter
1 tsp. water
Vanilla to taste

4 popsicle sticks or tongue depressors
4 crispy Granny Smith apples (or any other kind)

• In a large pot, melt down the caramels with the butter, water and vanilla. Heat the mixture until it is just about to boil. Then, let cool for 5 to 10 minutes. Cooling is important. If the mixture is too hot, the caramel will not stick to the apple.
• Take a tongue depressor and stick it into an apple, making sure you have a firm grip. Dunk the apple into the caramel to where the stick begins to come out of the apple. While dunking, make sure the entire apple is well drenched with caramel.
• Let the excess caramel drip off by holding the apple above the pot. Then, set on wax paper and let cool to room temperature.
• Eat right away or wrap in wax paper for later. You can do this by rubbing the wax paper lightly with butter to prevent sticking.

Michael is pouring the delectable liquid over sweet fruit in anticipation of another customer. Warm, melted chocolate dribbles onto the bamboo stick which is pierced with fruit. It flows down from the whole, bright, red strawberry to the pieces of orange, thick slices of banana, and apple wedge. Ultimately, all the fruit is covered in soft, drifting chocolate.

His motto bears the phrase, "If there is a heaven, its gardens bear chocolate covered fruit." It has only been a few months since Michael began his chocolate fruit cart business, aptly named the Luscious Chocolate Garden. The cart greets hordes of tourists in Woodstock, New York. More than two hundred miles miles north in Highgate, Vermont, Michael has come to serve the dessert in one of his favorite atmospheres, a Grateful Dead show.

Michael (Chocolate Garden Dipped Fruit). Photo: Mark Dabelstein

"There's something really spectacular when you're driving down the highway and in every direction you see folks that are going to the show," he proclaims. "It's just unbelievable. It's almost like the tail of a kite, watching it go down the highway. It's colors everywhere and flags and everyone's car is loaded up, and some of us are vending and some of us are just here for the show. It's the only show in the world that gets that happening.

"It's hard not to come back. That sounds very clichéed, but this is a whole very nomadic, self-empowered group here," explains Michael. "I think a long, long time ago it was considered a movement and now it's considered more like a carnival. The circus is coming to town. Entire generations of kids, they grew up and are now young adults. They grew up being brought to shows by their folks, I mean this is a real anomaly, a real unique thing."

Michael began serving chocolate covered fruit to Deadheads and tourists alike in the spring of 1995. An independent filmmaker, Michael started the business so he could raise money to continue making his movie, *Sacred Nation,* a film about environmental terrorism.

"I wanted to have something that was my own," he explains. "I don't have to answer to anyone but myself. Just me and my fruit. When I discovered that a vending spot had opened up in Woodstock, and it came time to figure out what I was going to vend, I thought of the normal things that everybody vends and that seemed like it wasn't really going to do much good.

"It sorta evolved

Luscious Chocolate Garden Dipped Fruit

"The beauty of this is that you're not really doing a recipe per se, you can do any combination that you want to do," says Michael.

*Experiment with fruit! "You would be really surprised what tastes good with chocolate," explains Michael. "Everyone likes the banana and strawberry concept, but there's thousands of fruits and anything with a little bit of chocolate added is only going to be that much better."

*You'll need a double boiler. "It doesn't have to be a fancy one that's bought," says Michael. "You can take two pots, one that's larger than the other, fill the bottom one with an inch of water. And then put the second pot in there. If possible, don't let the top pan touch the bottom pan or the water. Steam will work to heat it. Put the chocolate in the top pan and let melt."

Fresh fruit—try an amalgamation of fruits. Some suggestions: banana, orange, strawberry, apple, kiwi (though it does have a tendency to fall apart on the stick), pineapple

Bamboo shish kebab sticks

Chocolate—Use a good quality Belgian dark or milk chocolate. Or try experimenting with a mixture of milk chocolate and peanut butter. Use half of each for a nice mix. Michael suggests that you buy 100 percent chocolate made specifically for dipping. It can be bought in a grocery store. You can also use white chocolate, which, according to Michael is not really chocolate

"It's actually confectioner's sugar gone through a whipping process, it becomes chocolatelike," explains Michael. "It is similar in texture to chocolate, but the definition of chocolate is that it has to have cocoa in it and white chocolate has no cocoa in it at all.

→

"Good chocolate is very rich," he says. "If you love chocolate you can soak the fruit in it. The trick is to use the chocolate to enhance the taste of the fruit, so that you're tasting everything. But, if someone says, 'Kill me with chocolate,' I can kill a mortal man with chocolate."

• Slice the fruit and stick on a bamboo shish kebab stick. Dribble the chocolate over the fruit. "This is a very messy way to do it, but as Oscar Madison says, 'If you don't spill it all over yourself, you're not really enjoying it,'" Michael jokes. "If you're using a stick, take the sharp end and push it through the tip of the strawberry. I always have the strawberry on the tip side so you're not eating onto the point, you're eating onto the dull side. Then I do strawberry, orange, banana and then repeat. Take an apple wedge with the skin side down, and use this as the last piece you put on, as the bottom piece, because it is the piece which has the most grip. This holds the fruit together a little bit more."

• After you have set up your fruit kebab stick and the chocolate is heated, dribble chocolate onto the fruit (don't dip, the fruit pieces could fall off and you'll probably have too much chocolate). If you would like the chocolate harder and less drippy, place it in the freezer after adding the chocolate. This will tighten the chocolate into a candy as opposed to leaving it melted as a syrup.

• Another option is to just put the fruit in a bowl and cover with chocolate. It will be much less messy. Either way, have fun!

out of wanting to take a candy apple and use that theory of having something on a stick. Then I thought chocolate with fruit. I've eaten a lot of chocolate and fruit trying to figure out what I thought is best. I've worked in a bakery but never like this. Actually, everyone that I spoke to while I was trying to learn told me that I was crazy because chocolate is very sensitive to work with."

And so the Luscious Chocolate Garden was born. Now, Michael loves his new business in Woodstock, a community of artisans and creators.

"Having grown up in New York City, I like being around trees. I would say Woodstock is truly an artistic community, and not all communities are artistic communities. You've got to give it credit for that, because it's not easy being an artistic community these days. It has a lot of art happening, a lot of creativity, a lot of crafts, a lot of skills, and the world doesn't leave a lot of room for this stuff anymore. Somehow this has sort of stayed true. Now it's generations."

It's the ultimate dessert combination. Deadheads are amazed when they discover they can have a scoop of creamy, homemade vanilla ice cream on top of homemade banana bread. Although it was the first time they cooked at a Dead show, Jarrett and Christy (and their customers) couldn't have been happier.

"I had been wanting to make banana bread to sell at the Dead shows since the first time I went," says Christy. "I wanted to carry the banana bread in the basket and just wander around."

The two ended up staying in one spot to keep the frozen dessert on ice throughout the warm, Indianapolis day at the Deer Creek Music Center. Christy and Jarrett decided to make both desserts because Jarrett loves ice cream. It was the first batch he made in his parent's ice-cream maker.

"It's a lot of fun," he says smiling. "I just enjoy eating ice cream. I like fatty desserts, which is my problem. It's fun to make it yourself because it's something that most people assume you have to buy in the store.

"I've never tried to sell anything here before, and I had no idea what to expect," he continues. "The fun thing is just getting to talk to people as they go by.

Christy and Jarrett (Banana Bread and Ice Cream).
Photo: Mark Dabelstein

"Our plan wasn't to make money at all, it was just to come out here. We're planning to give fifteen percent of everything we make away to something. Some kind of a social activism group for our community, for people, for kids who have it rough in the city. Money makes people weird. I think both of us have a really bad attitude toward capitalism. I don't like the way our commercial society takes advantage of us."

Both Jarrett and Christy live and work in Indianapolis. Jarrett just finished college and wants to work as a high school teacher, while Christy is a Volunteer-Resource Coordinator with Habitat for Humanity.

"I want to expose kids to different areas," explains Jarrett. "I grew up in a town that was all white and all middle class, and there was a lot of prejudice. If you can just expose kids, show them. Literature is a good way to examine your attitudes toward sexism and racism. You question your beliefs, and you start questioning the way you live your life. So many kids, especially kids who grew up middle class, they don't even question, they don't know there's anything wrong."

"Habitat for Humanity is an ecumenical Christian organization, which is open to everybody," says Christy. "We build houses for very low-income families. The families do sweat equity, which is labor on their house, so it's not just a giveaway. We have sponsors and volunteers that build and then they buy the house on a no-interest mortgage and they don't have a down payment. They do their labor instead of a down payment. It meets the needs of a population that no one else is focusing on. These people cannot own a house any other way because there's nothing out there for them. They can't get a mortgage. Nobody will give them one because they don't make enough money."

Indiana Homemade Vanilla Ice Cream
Makes 3 quarts of ice cream

*Needed—An ice-cream maker, electric or manual

4 eggs
2 15 oz. cans condensed milk
1 cup sugar
1 cup whipping cream
1 Tb. vanilla

Approximately 1 1/2 quarts of milk
1 bag ice
1 1/2 cups salt

• Mix together the eggs, condensed milk, sugar, whipping cream and vanilla.
• Pour the mixture into the internal container of the ice-cream maker. Fill approximately 2 quarts of milk up to the container's fill line.
• Put the top on the internal container and fit it into the external tub. Fill the tub with ice cubes and salt, layering the two. Keep adding ice and salt as the machine cranks.
• This takes about 20 minutes with an electric ice-cream maker. Enjoy the creamy decadence!

Reaching most every continent, Christy says the organization is coming up to the forty-thousandth house they've built for low-income families since 1976. Helping this community meet one of their most basic needs makes Christy happy.

"I really enjoy working with them. I work with all the families that are there, just organizing people and making sure they know what they're doing, that they're taken care of. I really enjoy talking with the families and seeing why they are where they are, and what they need. It's easy to come from a middle-class society and not understand what's going on in low-income families and just think you know everything. It's been really good to have a chance to talk to people. They are people, and that's another thing. Middle-class society tends to consider them less than human. I've heard their stories and have gotten to see how they work and see their families. I'm a better person for it. I've learned from it.

"There's a world beyond the self, there's more to life than just making sure you or your family is okay, there's the broader world and at least the broader community in which you live," she explains. "There are poor people in every community, and there are poor people in crisis in every community. It's not like you have to look at your whole world, you can just look in your own neighborhood or your own community and see that there are people in need. I've really been studying this phenomenon of people giving, voluntary action for the public good. The phenomenon of why people go beyond the self and give beyond the self has a lot to do with the good feeling they get from doing something for other people. Sometimes it's guilt, sometimes it's God, if they have a religion, sometimes they have to do charity work. But people really care about other people.

"There's probably a lot of philanthropy here," she says of the scene. "There is a lot of begging going on, which is not bad. In Western society, people think of begging as a nasty thing, but in the East, begging used to be part of society. It's the way that religious monks lived, it's a blessed thing. I wouldn't consider the people who are begging for a Miracle to be monks, and I'm not sure they're on a journey toward a higher plane, but they might be, I'm not one to say. And I'm not sure it would work in any other concert system. But then there's other stuff going on, people asking for change so they can buy something. People asking for food, all that swapping that's going on. It's a whole economy here."

Yummy 'Nana Bread
Makes 1 loaf

WET INGREDIENTS
3 mushed up bananas ("The best bananas, of course, are the ones that are really old and have dots," says Christy)

1 egg
1/4 cup butter, melted (about 4 Tbs.)
DRY INGREDIENTS
1 cup sugar
1 1/2 cups flour. Wheat flour gives the bread an interesting taste.
1 tsp. salt
1 tsp. baking soda

• In separate bowls, mix the wet and the dry ingredients together. Combine both bowls and mix with a mixer or by hand. If the mixture appears too dry, adding a few tablespoons of organic apple juice can help. Grease the pans and pour in the batter.
• Bake in a preheated oven at 350° for an hour. Do the toothpick test, make sure it is golden brown on top.

On the morning of the last show at Soldier Field in Chicago, Dave's bus is parked in front of one of the parking lot's footbridge entrances. As people flow over the bridge, they instantly see his bus. A large sign next to the vehicle which advertises his yummy Elephant Ear treats is recognizable. Even more familiar is the ten-foot-tall, dark maroon, Victorian style addition (complete with shingles), that is attached to the top of his bus.

Dave's larger than life vehicle is a '77 Volkswagen with the exterior decorated in red, white, blue and black, interspersed with the occasional Escher interpretation. Constructed entirely out of recycled cedar, the wooden structure allows Dave a home away from home. Inside, he can hang out on the ground level or on the bed elevated high in the structure. Peering through the two Plexiglas skylights installed in the ceiling offers a perfect view of the deep, blue sky which emits a soft lighting into the bus.

The year 1996 will mark the tenth year that Dave's bus has ventured out on tour. For almost a decade, Dave has spent the weeks between tours working on the bus while living in Salyer, California, a small town of two hundred people in the Trinity National Forest. The nearest stoplight is sixty miles away.

"It's actually a product of sheer and absolute boredom," he explains, laughing. "I have nothing better to do with myself, we spend a lot of time alone and you gotta have a hobby."

The whole package amounts to a huge attraction, which is why Dave has also spent the

Dave (The Elephant Ear People). Photo: Mark Dabelstein

The Elephant Ear People
Serves 2

"I like to think of it as eating a whole box of cereal all at once."—Dave on Elephant Ears

Oil, any kind ("But not motor oil." Dave says, laughing.)
Vegetable will work fine
2 flour tortillas, any kind, any size

POSSIBLE TOPPINGS

Sugar
Cinnamon
Jelly
Chocolate
Ice cream
Fluff and Oreo cookies

- How big you make your elephant ears is only limited by the size of your pan, so cook accordingly.
- In a saute pan, wok or skillet, pour in an inch of oil. Heat the oil, drop in a tortilla and deep-fry. Flip and let cook until just light brown and crispy. (If it burns, you'll know; it'll turn black). Drain the oil off and let sit on a paper towel.
- Sprinkle sugar, cinnamon and any other toppings on top. Dave maintains they're best when eaten warm.
- Try one Indian style. Make chapatis by adding fresh garlic and pepper. (Dave says it's a favorite of Ganesh, the Hindu elephant God.) This probably won't make the best dessert, so use the chapatis in another dish. Try it with Chef Stef's Chickpea Chapatis on page 69.

last ten years letting his bus be the background for parking lot pictures and the talk of most every town he rolls into.

"Most people like it," he says. "It's really weird, it's almost like a big litmus test of how people are. It's if you ever want to find out where all the cops are and all the cool people are in any given area. So we like to smile for the satellite pictures as they go by, and wave to the policemen.

"I have a home and a job, this is just my summer thing. Usually it takes about three months every year in the wintertime to actually get it all together. It has taken a few shots, but it gets repainted and redone every year. Every year, I take the motor out, rebuild the whole engine, go through the whole thing. I used to have money and no car, now I have a car and no money."

When on tour, Dave (with his dog, Freckles) makes Elephant Ears, a simple dish of frying flat bread or tortillas. His mom gave him the recipe and he has cooked it since 1993. In the past, Dave has made Indian tacos and various full dinners for everyone in the parking lot.

"Full dinners are too much work and you don't make as much money," he laments. "You don't really want to work too hard, because then it seems like a job. I just do it for fun, because it's enjoyable making good food for people, and it's enjoyable to have people hanging out and it's fun to watch people freak out when they walk by.

"Elephant ears are a traditional food," he explains. "People call them elephant ears, funnel cakes, sopaipillas. Known by different names all over the world, it's a common food for common people for centuries, for holidays and festivities. That's kind of what the Dead thing is like, so it fits right in."

Dave and his crew deep-fry the sugary dessert whenever the moment strikes them. People always appreciate the time they put into making food and vending on the Shakedown.

"I find that taking part in a laissez-faire open-air marketplace tends to keep things on a more even keel," he says. "I like relating to people, we're equals when we're vending, dancing and interacting with people in that way. I have fun creating the scene, it's like a big sculpture of humanity.

"The Dead actually did a benefit concert for Joseph Campbell at the Berkeley Community Theater. He studied the Dead culture and his theory was, once again, it's just another one of those recurring outbursts of humanity. People are going to get together and dance around and enjoy themselves. Joseph Campbell wrote all those books about how all the various religions have various common denominators, just like bowling clubs or the Masons. Whenever you get a bunch of people together with similar interests, things happen, it's probably some sort of vortex you might say."

At most every show he brings them to, Jeff Kay's Dank Bran and Bootylicious Blueberry Muffins sell out rather quickly. Because he and his muffin collaborator, Ben Fernandez, usually end up going to shows by public transportation, they can only bring two or three dozen.

The two brought their muffins to the spring '95 Philadelphia shows via the subway. This caused somewhat of a problem. "We did it with great difficulty!" exclaims Jeff. "Some didn't make it, but crushed muffins make a great snack during set breaks.

"I first sold muffins at Nassau Coliseum in spring of '94," he explains. "Since then I've sold them at Giants Stadium and at the Philly spring shows. We sold about forty on each of those runs and could have sold more had we been able to transport them. Originally we only made bran muffins, but in Philly we brought about a dozen blueberry which seemed to go over well. Many seemed shocked to see people selling something other than the usual burritos and beer.

"Deadheads always have great stories to tell and muffins always serve as good conversation starters. The high amount of vending is just one of many examples of how Deadheads form a community of their own. Nobody is looking to get rich (with the possible exception of the guys selling nitrous balloons for five

Dank Bran and Bootylicious Blueberry Muffins
Makes 12 muffins

*Needed—a muffin pan

13/4 cups whole wheat pastry flour
21/2 tsps. baking powder
2/3 tsps. salt
1 egg
3/4 cup milk (1/4 cup more if needed)
1/3 cup vegetable oil
1/5 cup honey
1/5 cup sugar
1 shot of love

FOR BLUEBERRY MUFFINS
Add 1 cup fresh or frozen blueberries to the batter
• Preheat the oven to 400°. Butter a 12-cup muffin pan.
• Mix the flour, baking powder and salt in a clean bowl. In another bowl, beat the egg with the milk, vegetable oil, honey and sugar and add to the dry ingredients, stirring until the batter is just barely mixed.
• Spoon the batter into the muffin tin. Bake for 15 to 20 minutes.

dollars each). Vending is done in a laid-back fashion with the emphasis on selling a good, useful product, not ripping people off."

Jeff began listening to the Dead when he was fifteen with the compilation album, *Skeleton's in the Closet.* He became even more intrigued as he kept listening.

"I first began to understand what the Dead are all about when my friend loaned me the album. To this day, the NFA ('Not Fade Away') into GDTRFB ('Goin' Down the Road Feelin' Bad') is one of my favorite pieces of recorded music. Other key moments in my 'Dead development' include my first show and the first time I heard the second set of '2-13-70,' which is the greatest jam tape I've ever heard. And, of course, the first 'Unbroken Chain!'

"There are a lot of bands with extremely talented players and a lot of bands willing to take musical risks. Very few, however, give you both. The Dead do. That combined with excellent songwriting with tremendous variety in styles and great covers is what makes the Dead so special."

Kind Crafts

❀ ❤ ❀

Veggie Sister Solar Candles

"We just brainstormed basically," says Melanie. "We sat down and thought about things that we both would have fun making."

Wax—Beeswax or plain wax. You can buy a block of wax from any arts and
    crafts store.
Crayons—Use many different colors (but without the paper outside, of course)
Mold shapes—Use household items like milk cartons, Pringle cans, things that
    have good shape. Pierce a hole in the bottom for the wick.
Wicks
Ice cubes
Decorations—Whole spices, flowers, leaves, crystals, beads, anything your little
    creative heart desires

1.—Break off wax pieces and melt them down. To do this, use a double boiler or a large pot and fill with water. Boil the water and then place a sauce pan (with the wax inside the pan) into the water. Add color by breaking off pieces or using whole pieces of different crayon colors (or one solid color).
2.—Choose a cool mold and place a wick in the middle of the mold's center. (Your wick is going to be as big as your container). Once the crayon-wax mixture is hot and melted, fill the mold with ice. Pour the mixture over the ice. Let sit to harden, then pour out the excess water.
3.—To add another color, repeat this process but use a different crayon color. When you pour in another color, the new color will fill in where the ice cubes were sitting during the first pouring. Each time you do this, make sure to shake the wax around to reach the bottom and sides of the mold.
4.—Place in the fridge to harden. Feel inside to see if it has hardened and then cut out of the mold. (You can't use the mold again, sorry!) Burn and relax.

Picture yourself hundreds of miles from home, driving down long stretches of new and unexplored highway, on your way to a Dead show. Passing state lines and various roadside attractions, you can hardly contain your excitement as your destination becomes closer. The scenery is new and exciting, but after numerous hours of sitting, boredom can easily set in.

Many Deadheads overcome the problem by listening to music, reading, writing, singing, sharing stories, drawing and working on crafts to sell at the show.

Most of the macrame bracelets and necklaces Barbara makes are fashioned driving from state to state on her way to shows. The art of weaving the light brown pieces of hemp twine into jewelry takes time, patience and a certain amount of meditation, which is why Barbara loves it. She enjoys the opportunity to focus while traveling or just sitting in the Lot.

"It's a good meditation for me," remarks Barbara. "Then to come here and put out the work and have people appreciate what I do, what I live for, I get high and happy making it and I get high and happy watching other people appreciate it. It keeps our bliss and happiness going around in one big circle.

"The music is the center point of the circle we live and work in because Jerry and the boys and everyone that works for them are putting the most out, creating and providing a life where we can be who we want to be, because life in Babylon does not provide that."

Barbara has been a regular on Dead tour since 1990 and loves the life that touring provides. She also loves working with hemp for it enables her to educate people about how the plant can save the planet.

"Hemp, being the earth's most renewable resource, can provide fuel, fiber, food and paper. Hemp is the way to making a more conscious effort to preserve our planet," she explains. "As a paper product, we can save the forests of the American Northwest by eliminating clear cutting. Hemp can produce four times as much paper in one acre than trees. The fuel is ecologically safer, the food provides more protein than any other plant besides the soybean, and the fiber is more durable, long lasting and less refined. Besides that, it is just so groovy to wear!

Barbara (Hemp Macrame Bracelet). Photo: Mark Dabelstein

Hemp Macrame Bracelet
Makes 1 bracelet

Macrame is the art of tying knots. There are many macrame designs but described here are steps to make a necklace using a simple knot around multiple strings.

Make a wish when you tie it on. When it comes off, it will come true!

NEEDED:

Hemp Twine—Can be ordered from the Ohio Hempery in Columbus, Ohio, (see Glossary for phone number) or you can use any thin string or embroidery floss. Each string will be very long, so you'll need a lot to start out with.

Beads, shells, anything you want to put on your bracelet. Use anything of significance that dangles. The beads you use are your own creation.

Embroidery floss to add color—Substitute a string of embroidery floss for hemp twine.

Something to hook the end of the string while weaving. Use your toe or a hook or your shoe, anything stable. Barbara doesn't recommend using safety pins because they pull on the fabric they're pinned to.

*Note—To keep the strings from tangling, an option is to take each string and neatly wrap with a rubber band, undoing the band as you need more slack.

1. Barbara says you can use multiple strings to make your hemp jewelry. Described here is the method for using 4 strings.

2. Measure out 8 to 10 times more string than the finished piece will be. Now you will have 4 very long strings.

3. Hold the strings by their ends so they are nice and even. Make a small loop at the end and knot securely (See Diagram A). This loop will serve as the bracelet's clasp, so make it small enough to fit around the bead (or knot) you will use as the clasp.

4. Hook the loop on to something sturdy (a boot, your toe, etc.) and begin weaving. Another option is to take an additional piece of string and tie that into the loop to create a second loop. Then, attach that second loop to something sturdy. This way, the first loop, which will be the bracelet's clasp, can be smaller. Use whatever works for you.

5. Weave the outside strings under each other, alternating outside strings and adding beads anywhere along the way until you get to the end (See Diagrams B and C). The two middle strings (which aren't really weaved, but rather, are weaved over) will give the necklace width and bulk. Again, these middle strings are not weaved, they are simply wrapped around by the two outside strings. Neither of the outside strings will be wrapped, they will always stay out of the knot.

↓

6. Continue weaving until you get to the end. Then, take the middle strings and the outside strings and tie them together. You also may finish with a braid which will complement the macrame pattern.

7. Whether or not you braid them all together, tie the end into a big, fat, round knot (then place a bead on if you like). That knot (or bead) can be used to secure the loop on the other end (the loop you began with), therefore creating a clasp. Now, you have a very styly, new piece of homemade jewelry!

A   B   C

"In the beginning, I vended first and foremost to get from show to show and to take care of myself," says Barbara. "Now, first and foremost, I vend because there is no other work I'd rather be doing. No other job that satisfies the soul quite like this one. I mean, what other job do you know of where you get off work and hop on a plane into dreamy space?

"The kind free spiritual people here at shows opened the door for me to the music, which will keep me here for life. I wouldn't understand what life is worth, I wouldn't believe all the things we can do if it wasn't for the Grateful Dead."

Late afternoon sunlight pours waves of red and orange onto Amy and the woman's hair she is weaving. Using her fingers to wrap each thin, colorful string around and around the braid, Amy continually alternates between colors. First, three knots of brown, then yellow, then black and then a few beads. She wraps the hair until color stretches all the way to the end, taking along with it an assortment of designs, loops and beads.

Amy is a skilled artisan. She turns hair into a band of colors, sometimes using hemp string, other times embroidery floss. For the last five years, giving people (and the occasional dreaded dog) hair wraps has paid for Amy's tour expenses, let her set her own hours and given her the opportunity to work anywhere around the country she wants.

"It's so much better than a nine to five job. I get to wake up at twelve, work in the sunshine and never have to be at a desk." Amy smiles. "I like being on the road, that's why I like traveling with the Dead. I can be my own boss and it's cash. I can set up shop anywhere, so if I need money real quick I can just do a hair wrap, get twenty bucks and eat. I'm self-sufficient, plus, I like being around people, meeting people, and hair wrapping is so good for that, it makes me feel good. It's a creative outlet. It's just a perfect way of living."

Amy learned how to wrap hair from friends in Gainesville, Florida. Then she began wrapping on tour and realized she could do it anywhere she went, including spring break in Florida and Saturday market in Oregon.

Amy believes hair wraps are like hair jewelry, a symbol of freedom and expression for the hair. For Amy, the fun part is creating them.

Amy (Hair Wrap). Photo: Mark Dabelstein

"It's kind of like therapy, staring at colors all day, talking to different people. People sometimes tell me their life story," she explains. "Sometimes little kids get it done and they just love it and it makes me feel good too. It's fun knowing that it's going to be traveling all over the world. There's going to be hair wraps that I made, each lasting up to eight months everywhere around the country. I have walking art all over the world. In Hawaii I did hair wraps on girls from Japan and on tour I've done wraps on people from all over the country. A lot of people are going to be looking at it, checking it out. It's a finished tangible thing."

In 1990 Amy graduated from Florida State University with a degree in communications. Since then, she has spent her time on Dead tour and going to Rainbow Gatherings, traveling alone and with friends.

How to Hair Wrap

"I make each one different depending on the colors, but I have some patterns that I do a lot because I know they look good," says Amy. "Sometimes I'll do color for about an inch and then have a middle spacer color like yellow or white and I'll just do three knots of that color.

"Some people look tribal, and some people look like party people and it depends on the colors they pick, it depends on my mood. If I'm in a really good mood, my wraps will be really good."

YOU'LL NEED:

Embroidery thread (lotsa colors!)—use six times the length of the hair you're wrapping

Scissors

Beads

A friend's hair

Pony tail holder (Scrunchies work great! See page 147 for a recipe on how to make them)

Patience

- *—The amount of hair you use in the wrap is dependent on the type of hair you have to work with and how big you want the wrap to be. Common spots to place the wrap are at the bottom of the scalp, behind the ear or the top of the hair.*
- *—Experiment! "Make up knots," says Amy.*

1. Take a small amount of hair (about the width of one and a half pencils stuck together) and braid it, making sure all the hairs are straight, the braid is tight and the braid runs all the way up to the scalp. Tie a hair elastic to the end of the braid and pull the rest of the hair away from the braid with a scrunchie.

2. Pick out 4 or 6 colors of embroidery thread or hemp string. Described here will be the procedure to wrap with 4 strings. Each string should be about 6 times as long as the hair you're wrapping.

3. Hold all the strings together, then evenly tie one big, tight knot at the very top of the braid, right up to the scalp. Push this knot up against the hair so it is sturdy. This will act as a safety latch. (See Diagram A) Make sure there is an even amount of string on both sides. (You'll have 8 symmetrical strings hanging down.)

4. Now, begin to wrap. This takes patience, so stick with it. Use only one string at a time, so if you are using 4 strings (doubled over makes 8 strings), the other 7 will stay with the braid as you wrap. When you do 1 string, you wrap it around the other 7 strings and with the braid.

5. There are many techniques and patterns to hair wrapping, but starting with a basic 4-knot is easiest.

6. To start, begin with one string. Take the string and make the shape of a 4 by pulling it out over the top of the braid, then under the braid and then through the hole you made by pulling it out, so it looks like a 4. After each loop, pull tight. (See Diagram B)

7. Continue for as many knots as you like, picking up other colors as you go along. This should create a spiral pattern. Alternate strings when you want to change colors to create a pattern. Remember to pull tight each time you make a knot so that it is secure.

8. To add a bead, find one with a good size hole. Cut a piece of embroidery thread about 4 inches long. Fold it in half, then take the braid and the remaining strings and wrap them with the string. Slide the bead on the 4-inch thread and pull the strings through the other side of the bead hole. Slide the bead up the braid.

9. To finish the wrap, tie the strings together into a really good knot so it is secure, or braid the ends, adding any small beads, charms and bells onto the very end. Your new hair wrap will be stiff for a week or so until it begins to soften when bathing and with wear. A hair wrap is like having a hair tie built into your hair, especially if there is a bead at the end. Carefully use the wrap to tie your hair back.<None>

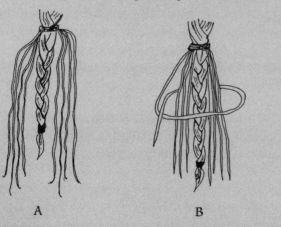

A   B

"I travel around alone all the time," she says. "It's freedom, knowing that if any situation isn't good for my peace of mind that I could get out of it if I want to. Different people have different things to teach and I have things to teach people. When I travel around by myself I can meet a variety of people, and I like teaching hair wraps too.

"I have about five different families that I travel with and I always know I can go with them if I want to. Being a good rider is important, offering money, offering something, contributing. It's fun, I would recommend going on Dead tour to anyone who wanted to travel and meet people. It's just how you learn. It's graduate school."

The sight is breathtaking. Men and women clad in long skirts and dresses, twirling in circles, flowing with the air and concentrating deeply on the music. For some, it is meditation; others a joyous celebration of life. Whatever the occasion, the vision is beautiful, for as they spin, so do their clothes. Yards of frayed, sun drenched lace trims soft, delicately patterned cotton dresses that sweep the floor in soft circles and drift ever so slowly, so gently in tune with the air.

It is exquisite to watch and just as intense to do. Exchanging energy with those around you, the entrancing meditation of moving around and around with the music simply feels good. When spinning, wearing a long, flowing dress can help keep balance and focus.

When Elska makes her dresses she knows people will appreciate the love and work she has put into sewing them, with spinning in mind.

"Dresses are a whole different thing for me, just because I spin and I make the dresses very full for spinning," Elska explains. "When I see someone spinning in one of my dresses, it's really intense, because they're really beautiful.

"People like to have the full dresses to spin. It balances them. And just to have that flow

Elska (Hair Scrunchies). Photo: Mark Dabelstein

beneath you. For a lot of people, spinning is very spiritual. Like when you're spinning sometimes, you're taken on a totally different plane. I don't do drugs at all, and spinning gets me spiritually high, intensely spiritually high," she says with a smile. "I can't spin without a dress. It's familiar, it just balances me."

Elska started creating dresses, hair scrunchies and jumpsuits after picking up different sewing techniques from friends. Now a full-time craft, sewing is gratifying for Elska, it's an activity she can pour herself into.

Elska's Hair Scrunchies

Fabric—cut 29 inches by 5 inches
Scissors
Thread spool, any color
Needle

Crocheting needle
Safety pin
Elastic—10 inches long and 1/2 inch wide
Invisible thread

1. Take a piece of fabric and cut it 29 inches long and 5 inches wide. (Diagram A) First, sew the sides (the width) together backward. The pattern will be inside-out and you'll be creating a long tube with the fabric. (Diagram B) Using a crocheting needle, pull the fabric right-side-out so the pattern is now facing you. (Diagram C)

2. Bring the ends together with the pattern facing each other and sew together, leaving an inch open for the elastic.

3. Stick a safety pin through the end of the elastic and pull it through the scrunchie.

4. Now take the ends of the elastic and tie them in a slip knot. Pull as hard as you can so it is really tight and will not come undone. Don't sew the elastic together, it will always break and thread can't withhold the elastic's stretch. (Diagram D)

5. Fold the open sides under about half an inch and sew up with invisible thread.

For a fluffier scrunchie, cut the fabric 40 inches by 5 inches and make the elastic longer.

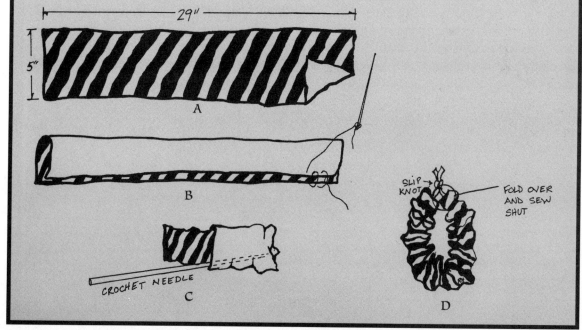

"I really like to drown myself in my sewing," she says. "Sometimes it takes me a little while to get into it, because it's a head space, but once I get into the mode, I don't stop. I stay up till two and three in the morning and just sew. In kind of a weird way, it's like meditation. You're not thinking about anything, it's just creating. . . you're creating something.

"I was going through rough times last year and sewing was my therapy, I just drowned myself in everything. That was all I did. I sewed twenty-four hours a day. So I took something negative and it came out really beautiful and positive."

Elska had been going to see the Dead since 1990 and loves it deeply. Her first show was a moving experience.

"Basically, the first show I ever went to, I was in the second row and everybody was dancing," remembers Elska. "There wasn't a single person in the whole coliseum not dancing and no one cared how anyone else danced. I finally let loose and the music took over my body. I've never had that happen. Literally, my hands, my feet, my arms, everything moved to the beat of the music. It was just extremely intense. The Grateful Dead's music just takes over your body.

"In a lot of ways, Jerry is somewhat divine to me because he can take me so high. I mean he's made me totally break down in tears, so many times. I feel like the Grateful Dead has this crystal ball, and they know what's going on in everybody's lives. Every show I go into, they play the songs that totally deal with what is going on in my life and they help me work through things. They don't solve my problems, but it's kinda like therapy, like maybe, give me a direction, help me understand things more.

"Music wise, I have the utmost respect for every single member in the band. They're incredible musicians. When they get on stage, they're connected. I don't want to say I favor one more than the other, but Jerry's voice basically soothes my soul.

"I really want my children to be able to experience this, because it's such an important part of my life. Once you're on tour, it's even beyond the music, it's the friendship, it's the unity between people. It's just an intense place. I've learned more in my years on Grateful Dead tour then I learned my whole life before that. I've learned a lot."

What would a Grateful Dead show be without scores of dancing, spinning, twirling tie-dye clad people to excite and captivate the mind? Psychedelics or not, visions of these multicolored patterns can catapult any mind into a parachute of colors, which also seems to go along particularly well with the music.

The Althea crew, Sleepy, Dave, Joe, Jeanna and Julie thought they'd let everyone try their hand at tie-dying, so they brought some buckets, white T-shirts and lots of dye to the parking lot outside of The Omni in Atlanta and went to work making some killer dyes in an exceptionally short period of time.

The Althea crew spans the country. They're from all over the East Coast but converged in Philadelphia early in the tour so they could travel together.

"We got together by friends of friends of friends and we all met, hooked up, and kicked off on tour," says Dave. "We've all been getting into shows. I'd have to say this is the best tour I've ever been on because of family. The Althea family."

The bunch are dubbed the Althea crew to pay tribute to the multicolored Ford van they travel in, also named Althea. In addition, the five also travel with four dogs, two of them puppies.

"It's good at times, but it's kinda hectic at times," says Jeanna who owns one of the puppies. "You have to constantly watch them. We're having a potty training problem with the puppies."

"Problem?" exclaims Dave. "You mean disaster! Never have I traveled with such unobedient canines!"

"But they're puppies." Jeanna laughs.

The Althea Family (Tie-dye). Photo: E. Zipern

The group digs tour but has had financial troubles on their travels.

"I think sometimes Dead tour can be too much into money," says Dave. "You almost forget what it's all about because you're just stressing. We've been so stressed about money lately, and it's ridiculous. We're making ourselves miserable over money, and that's why we came here, to get away from all that. Sometimes it's kind of a pain, but then on the other hand, it's hard to make money any other way.

"My favorite thing about Dead tour is probably the spontaneity," he continues. "Life is such a roller coaster on Dead tour, but it's so worth it because the highs are so high, and other than friends getting arrested, there really aren't too many lows."

149

Do Your Own Dyes!

"It's all in the pleat, how big you make the pleats and where you put them. Use decent dyes, use them properly, use your imagination, and you've got it down. Also, find a forgiving mother who doesn't mind you ruining laundry," says tie-dye aficionado, Mike Walsh.

YOU'LL NEED:

Soda ash—Can be bought from Dharma Trading Co., but it can also be found in swimming pool supply stores.

Lots of water close by—A big laundry work-sink works great.

Various squeeze bottles—Try using plastic mustard bottles. You can twist the nozzle to just the right amount, but clean them out well first.

Dyes—The Dharma Trading Co. is one place to order dyes from. (See Resources and Notes) You'll need some nice colors, so pick wisely and order their free catalog. (What you're exactly looking for are fiber reactive dyes—Procion is the major brand.)

100% cotton white T-shirts (cotton takes the dye better). Don't be afraid to dye other stuff. Try pants, socks, bras, underwear, etc.

Rubber gloves so your hands don't get stained. Tie-dye wiz Mike Walsh recommends against them, but they can be used. Mike's Cafeteria Lunch Tray Trick minimizes dye on hands (though getting dye on your hands is virtually unavoidable). Keep readin' for more info!

Rubber bands—Use rubber bands to create patterns. Twine can also be used to make neat patterns.

Plastic wrap.

Synthrapol—Mike dubs this substance, "Liquid of the gods." "I wouldn't even think about doing a post dye rinse wash without this," he says.

1. For the best outcome, Mike recommends prewashing the shirts. "Various fabric treatments and sizings are still present on many of the shirts that you will purchase," he explains. "Wash like you would any other T-shirts with a decent quality detergent and a full rinse cycle. The washing and drying will also shrink the shirts to their final shape so that your dyeing will be accurate."

2. Begin by preparing a pre-treat/soak. Add 1 cup soda ash into a gallon of lukewarm water. You'll end up with a lot more solution than you'll need, so dye lots of other stuff if you're in the mood.

3. Soak the shirts for 5 minutes, then wring out well, making very sure all excess liquid has been removed.

→

TYING—COURTESY MIKE WALSH

1. First, select your tying area carefully. The soda ash solution will damage wood and many finishes. Select something like a Formica table, or carefully cover your surface with a big, thick piece of plastic. The surface should be big enough to completely spread out the shirt and have some room to work.

2. Two people are recommended to do this. One to pleat the fabric and one to apply the rubber bands or twine. You can do this alone, but it isn't much fun, and two people go much faster.

3. Folding/pleating/gathering the fabric is where the real art of tie-dyeing comes in. Your pattern depends exclusively on where the dye ends up, and this is dependent on how you gather your fabric and how you apply the dye.

4. The size of your pleats or folds will determine how deep the dye goes. The "shorter" you make your pleats in height, the easier it will be for the dye to penetrate and the less white in your shirt. Likewise, "taller" pleats will leave more white in general because more of the the shirt will be deep in the bundle.

5. You won't actually dye the shirts for a couple of steps, but we've described the coloring for patterns here because the folding, tying and dyeing of the shirts all go hand in hand.

*Note—Generally colors that are next to each other on the color wheel (red, purple, blue; red, orange, yellow; green, blue, purple) go together very well. But feel free to experiment. Black has a nice effect if you can carefully avoid bleeding. The ties or rubber bands will help to keep the dyes from smearing together, so place your ties wherever you want to change colors. If you want to have a large section of a single color, make sure to have ties about every few inches, just so it's easier to handle the bundle.

MORE DYEING NOTES

*Most patterns are one or a combination of the following three techniques: Spirals, lines and bunches.

*Dye penetration is dependent on pleat height. It's 80 percent pleat height, 10 percent amount of dye and 10 percent tightness of the tie.

*Excessive dye penetration can be a symptom of excessive dye application and/or loose tying. All factors interact, so experience will guide you after a few bunches of shirts.

*See the Cafeteria Lunch Tray Trick on page 153 before proceeding to dye.

Spirals: Also known as swirls, the classic "dye" you see around. Making this is easier than you would ever imagine. Spread the shirt out on a surface and pinch the fabric at the location from which you want the spiral to begin (the center, the pocket, etc.). Now, put that pinched fabric between the tines of a fork and twist. The shirt will pull in as you twist and with a little bit of attention to keeping your pleat height roughly consistent, you will end up with a bundle that looks a little like a cinnamon bun.

To color, the usual technique is to divide the round bundle into wedges, like pieces of pie. Color each piece a different color. Repeat on the backside—you can use the same colors, or different colors or one color. The effect will be single color swirls, swirls with alternating colors, and a single color swirl against a solid background (respectively).

Lines: These are the most basic, and most versatile, of all patterns. Make your first pleat, then gather in the direction that you want your lines to go. Feel free to wander all over the shirt. You can make semicircles, hearts, random directions, whatever.

The V design shirts are nothing more than a shirt that was folded once vertically, then gathered toward the shirtsleeve. One way to visualize things is to watch a portion of the fabric move—when you apply the dye across that section of pleats (or to be clear, perpendicular to the pleat ridge), the dye line will go exactly where you watched the portion of fabric go when you gathered. Like the spiral, you will apply the dye across the pleats and then color the top and bottom in whatever combination you want.

Bursts:These are formed by grabbing the shirt at a particular point and lifting. As you lift, you gather the fabric into pleats and tie/rubber band the package into sections. This will create sunburst patterns. These can work very well with screened shirts just as line derived patterns can.

More complex things to try include folding the shirt before starting the pleating and combining patterns. For example, by folding the shirt in half before starting a spiral you will get two duplicate spirals that merge together. You can also combine patterns by doing things like pleating the bottom and then twisting the remainder of a shirt into a swirl. Or do both folding and combining. If you fold the shirt vertically, pleat the bottom in a line to form a V when unfolded and gather the bundle together with a spiral twist, you can make a fairly neat heart pattern. Really.

1. Prepare the dye according to package instructions. Mike recommends doing this as far from your tied shirts as possible.

"Fiber reactive dye does get into the air and travels farther than you would ever believe. It's surprising what you will find that has been accidentally dyed by drifting powder and eventual moisture. Mixing the dye outside is the best bet, but if you have to mix inside, wear an inexpensive mask. Your lungs are natural fibers just like cotton and you wouldn't want to shock a surgeon some day with purple lungs.

"Keep the soda ash and mixed dye separate until they mix on the shirt. Since the soda ash is already in the shirts, there isn't any need to mix in any here. Once the dye and soda ash mix, the usable life of the dye is very short. By doing this two-step process (a) soak the shirts in soda ash and (b) apply the dye; we found the dye lasted up to a week instead of about two days for a pre-mixed solution of dye and soda ash."

Wash your hands!

2. Now apply the dye to the T-shirt. Do this with a squeeze bottle that has a good, straight stream. Create your design! (See above.)

The Cafeteria Lunch Tray Trick

Mike recommends digging up cafeteria lunch trays to minimize the amount of dye that will get on your hands. Put the shirt bundle on the tray, apply the dyes and then carefully flip or rotate the bundle as needed until all the dye has been applied. "If you are careful about rotating/flipping/accidentally moving the bundle, you will never smear the dyes into each other," he says. "You can then wipe your hands on a rag, grab the shirt bundle with the piece of plastic wrap you are going to use, wrap the shirt tightly and then wipe the tray with your rag. (By the way, the rag gets pretty psychedelic.) This works great! I've yet to hear of or see a better system than using lunch trays."

3. When you're done creating your design, put the shirt (or each shirt that you use) in plastic wrap. Mike says it's easier and better for wrapping "long" bundles you'd never find a bag for. Be absolutely sure it is wrapped airtight and don't wring out any of the liquid. The dye must stay wet to be active.
4. Set in a warm place for 24 to 48 hours. "The colors seem more brilliant after forty-eight," says Mike.
5. Now it's time to take the shirt out of the bag. Before undoing the rubber bands and checking out the psychedelic patterns you just created, put the shirt under cold water until the water running off becomes clear. With the shirt still under the cold water, undo/cut the rubber bands. (You'll be amazed by how much dye flows off!)
6. Synthrapol—Mike recommends keeping a bucket of warm-hot water with a good dose of Synthrapol in it nearby. Put a shirt in there as you cold rinse the next shirt. When that shirt is ready to go in the Synthrapol bucket, pull the first one out and rinse it in warmish water until it runs clear.
7. Again, a lot of dye will come out. "The warm water helps the remaining dye come out and the Synthrapol does a pretty good job of avoiding backstaining. At this point the shirt is pretty 'clean' but will backstain to some degree on itself and other shirts if you dawdle. If you can put them out on a clothesline until the rest are rinsed, do."

↓

8. When all are rinsed, put them in a washing machine on a heavy cycle with warm water and a good dose of Synthrapol. "Wash at least once this way, and maybe twice if you are a real stickler for a white background. After you dry the shirt you should have no further problems with bleeding, but wash with darks the next few times just to be safe."

"We used this method for three years and had remarkable 'whiteness' in our shirts," he says. "Synthrapol is the real key, and putting the washing machine to work when you've manually rinsed out all you can.

"We (and many others) use Laundromats to do the postrinse wash. Please be kind and run the machine one time empty after finishing to give it a real nice rinse out—it's only a few quarters and it saves the next person some potential grief."

Also, bleach does a good job of cleaning the dye off your hands.

CLEAN UP

The Dhama Trading Co. suggests neutralizing the soda ash with vinegar before you pour it down the drain (soda ash raises the pH level of water). Add vinegar until pH neutral, then pour down drain.

Dharma has heard of problems regarding cleanup, so the following notes are worth mentioning. We know how damaging it would be to our oceans, lakes and rivers if we tie-dyed in these bodies of water and not in a work sink. Please remember, the dyes are better off being dumped in the sewer than directly into the environment.

Mike's Story. . .

"I first got started by a buddy of mine (Mike F.) who was a Resident Assistant at my college back in '87. He sort of introduced me to the 'Boyz' and tie-dyeing at the same time and I haven't been the same since," Mike explains. "Every few weeks we would walk through the dorms and collect up clothing friends wanted dyed. We'd take those and however many shirts we could scrape up money for and head on down to Mike F.'s room. By the spring of that year we were pretty good, but we couldn't remember the original color of the carpet he had rolled out on his floor.

"I kept dyeing for the next year or so between school and home in NJ, always having a blast and coming up with new designs. And experience was the best teacher. The last batch was in the summer of '89 and it was the best yet. Several times I've thought about playing around again, but there's a million other projects pulling me around. Collecting soundboard tapes has proven to be a lot less messy and time consuming, so I'll keep rolling with that for a while."

The nine small glass bottles look simply elegant. Filled with scented herbal lotions, they sit perched on a short, carved wooden table, while Mer hangs near them, laughing with friends and waiting for the show to begin. By the end of the day, Mer has nearly sold out, though she says she's not much of a salesperson. The herbal lotions, made with all natural ingredients have been selling on their own, enticing those shopping the Shakedown outside of the Seattle Memorial Stadium. Mer learned to make the herbal blend with friends in Tofino, British Columbia.

"I learned from people up in Tofino last summer and then by herbal body books," explains Mer. "I've been making them for about a year, but I've only made them for myself. Seattle is the first time I sold them."

Mer, her family and her friends use the lotions almost every day to moisturize, heal and protect dry skin, for sunburns, split lips, rashes, diaper rashes, burns, bruises, swelling, scabs.

"It's fun, and I know what I'm putting on my skin and I know they're going to work if I'm using them for a certain purpose," Mer says. "I know they're going to heal me. I can make them smell the way that I want and I don't have to buy into the whole cosmetic thing. It's all natural and I know exactly what is in there.

"I think if people knew, if they trusted the herbs, then they'd be more than happy to make them because they're totally simple to do, but people are so interested in the whole cosmetic industry. My mom uses my stuff, her friends use my stuff. I think that everyone is sort of leaning to this natural, organic thing, it's the trend."

Ever since 1990, Mer has been leaving Canada and hitting the road for shows in the States. The closest venue from British Columbia is Seattle's Memorial Stadium, just an hour and a half south down I-5 from the B.C. border.

"I can't imagine the Grateful Dead coming over to Canada," Mer considers. "When you cross the border, when you get to Seattle, you know that you're in the States. It's definitely a different feeling. I think there's more attitude, or confidence, it's exciting. I love visiting the States, and I've always had a great time.

"If you go on tour and you come back to Canada, it's a totally different place to come home to. It's a weird thing, because you are

(Mer's Salve and Massage Oil). Photo: E. Zipern

Mer's Salve and Massage Oil
Makes about 5, 12 ml. bottles

2 to 3 cups dried herbs—Try: chamomile (flowers), comfrey (root), burdock (root), kelp, peppermint (leaves) (Mer says these herbs are similar in their healing properties and therefore compliment each other, though you may add any favorite herb.)
White wine, enough to completely saturate the herbs
2 cups olive oil
3/4 cup beeswax or less, depending on desired consistency (found at a craft or natural food store)
Several Tbs. hemp oil (you can get this from the Ohio Hempery)
1 cup apricot oil, almond oil, grape seed oil or a combination
2 cups vitamin E oil
Essential oils—vanilla, rose or any other oils you like
Glass jars, bottles, any container

TO MAKE THE SALVE:
1. Soak the herbs in white wine for several hours. The alcohol in the wine will extract the potency of the herbs. Add olive oil to this mixture and simmer gently in a glass pot until the smell of alcohol is replaced by the warm scent of the herbs. Don't let it get too hot, or it will burn. This should take about half an hour.
2. Drain the olive oil from the herbs. While the drained olive oil is still warm add the beeswax and allow it to slowly melt down. Then, add the remainder of the oils and also whatever essential oils you choose. "Certain oils are better for certain body parts," Mer says. "For example, vanilla and rose oil is for breasts and belly." While the salve is still liquid, pour into pots (jars), then let cool.

TO MAKE MASSAGE OIL:
After draining the herbs from the olive oil, pour the liquid into glass jars. The only difference between making the salve and the massage oil is that beeswax is never added to the massage oil mixture.

going to a different country for the whole experience, coming home to this total beauty other than cities and the highway. For me, it's coming back to old growth and ocean. My home is so beautiful!

"At the time, coming from suburbia, I had no idea what the shows were like. I knew a lot of people that had gone down, but it was definitely an eye opening experience for me, that there was this entire way of life that you could exist and be happy living that way, a total subculture. It was a very liberating thing, it definitely opened my eyes to a lot of other possibilities. It was just like major beauty and openness. It made me very happy, that's for sure.

"It's the unexpected, the people that you meet, just watching people, the beauty that I see, beautiful people from all over the place, people that are coming together for a common cause. It's easy, it's fun, it's exciting, it's okay."

Deadheads are famous for utilizing any method of transportation necessary to get to a Dead show. Known to take planes, buses, cars and trains, if there is a show in the vicinity, a Deadhead will be sure to find it. But, getting there isn't always that easy.

Unless you're prepared to act like a cabbie, driving into New York City presents disasters on a regular basis, as does parking. Public transportation is key, and for years, Deadheads in the New York, New Jersey Metropolitan area have made use of the region's public transportation system to get them to the Big Apple and into Madison Square Garden, the legendary venue situated atop Penn Station, New York City's largest train and bus depot.

Candace (Dream Catcher). Photo: Mark Dabelstein

When Candace goes to see the Dead or Phish at Madison Square Garden, one of her favorite modes of transport is to sit back, relax and take the train. An hour and a few stops from where she goes to school in New Brunswick, New Jersey, Candace digs the train scene. She remembers enjoying the hour of relaxation and conversation before her first Dead show.

"The first show I went to, we took the train, and it was very, very awesome," says Candace. "People were giving out food, hemp cookies, just hanging out, partying, and nobody had to worry about being the driver. We were all going to the same place on the train.

"It wasn't all about vending, it was about giving stuff away and sharing and everybody was excited. You could walk up and down all the cars and see all kinds of people and everybody was partying really hard. I met a lot of really nice people."

Candace's first show was at "The Garden" in 1991. Hearing about Dead shows for years, she finally went and was introduced to an atmosphere completely different from what she was used to, growing up in suburban New Jersey.

"Madison Square Garden was crazy because it was such a metropolitan show with all different kinds of people coming to check it out," she explains. "Going to a suburban high school, I had probably never seen so many different kinds of people as I experienced at that show. It was very nice, everybody was really cool, sharing joints. There were a lot of people from all different kinds of places, from far away, and I was kind of like, 'Oh, this Dead thing is something, these people are from far away.' Everybody was so energetic, dancing and dancing. I have never seen dancing like that in my life!"

Now before she goes to shows, Candace likes to bead, sew and weave in her kitchen while talking to friends, which is how she and her friend Elisabeth came up with their own version of a Dream Catcher. Since then, Candace has made them for family and friends to put over their beds to catch their dreams.

"My friend Elisabeth Coffey had one hanging in her room, and we were like, 'We can figure out how to make these,'" she says. "We just sat down on the front porch and figured it out. Lis kinda had the concept, and I applied it more. Hers was very random, and I got the whole geometrical thing down.

"They're a Native American tradition, and they're supposed to protect you while you sleep, to help catch evil spirits. What I found they do is they really catch your dreams and you can remember them more. If you have one by your bed and you wake up and you see it, you think about the dream you had last night, which is cool because so many people just don't think about that.

"It's a little bit different than anything else you might see on the Lot. It's cool because you're taking elements from your environment. You take a feather which is kind of like the wind, and twigs which is kind of like the earth. A lot of people like to use very fancy feathers, but I think it's good to use whatever is in your environment around you. Brumfus (New Brunswick) pigeons might not be that pretty, but it's what I'm surrounded by. It keeps you in touch with what is directly around you rather than buying feathers that are a little prettier."

Dream Catcher

"It was cool to see bartering and trading and handmade things that people put a lot of time and love into making. And food. . . if you're a vegetarian, then the Lot is the place to eat," says Candace. "It's not even so much for people to buy, but for people to just see, appreciate and have other stuff to show and trade."

WHAT YOU'LL NEED:
* This is a stuff lying around in the backyard type project, so use what you can find!*
A stick or branch that is fairly flexible and can be shaped into an oval or circle when bent.
      (Candace says that honeysuckle works great!)
Lots of string—can be hemp, embroidery thread, satin, anything fairly durable. (Bakery string is
      strong.)
Beads, shells, anything you want. Keep a sensational center bead in mind and save for the end.
Wire to tie the ends.
A feather (preferably one found in your area). Take a walk and check out the ground!

PROCEDURE
1. Take your stick or branch and gently bend it into a circle or oval. Tie the ends together with a piece of wire or something that is strong.
2. Then, take the string (you can do this in steps or with one long string) and wrap it around the stick in knots. (The idea is to tie 8 to 12 loop-knots around the circle you created.) You can make as many knots as you like, but keep in mind the more knots you use, the more intricate the design will end up, so start simple. (Diagram A) The knots should be the same size and distance apart. Plan ahead to ensure that spacing between each knot is even. This will create a more uniformly angled Dream Catcher. Space the knots about an inch apart and make sure the string between the knots isn't too taut. Leave a little slack when you tie the first knot. The knots should also be relatively small so they don't stick out. (One way to cover the knots is to put beads over them.)
3. After tying loops once around the circle and you are back at the first knot, tie a new knot to the slack you left. Then thread or loop the string through the first loop. (Diagram B) Once you loop around again to where you've just looped through, loop the first loop again so it looks like a sun (Diagram C).

⬇

4. The trick is where you begin a new concentric circle, you will have to loop twice.

5. To finish, once the loops and circles get very tiny, end your last concentric circle and thread through the center piece bead saved for the end. (Diagram D) Then tie from the point where you ended directly across. Tie your finishing knot.

6. Tie a feather at the bottom of the circle. Hang over your bed!

CANDACE'S MISCELLANEOUS ITEMS TO ADD TO THE DREAM CATCHER:

For those with nightmares, a sprig of lily of the valley ought to help. For those who have insomnia, try chamomile, lavender or rose. These may be tied onto the Dream Catcher or essential oils may be dabbed onto the twine. Also, a mixture of orange and lemon essential oils can be added to the twine used in making the Dream Catcher.

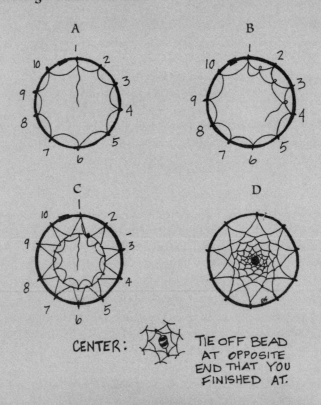

CENTER: TIE OFF BEAD AT OPPOSITE END THAT YOU FINISHED AT.

Sitting on a blanket next to the Last Supper Kitchen's food-laden table, Amanda, with her puppy, Samborini, by her side, is beginning to sew a large velvet pouch by hand. She is sewing because a man, camping in the parking lot three cars over just came by to commission her to make a large velvet pouch. Instead of exchanging money for the work, the two have opted to make a trade. For the pouch he'll give her a multicolored stained glass peace sign. Amanda loves that she can custom make her work for him in mind.

"It's a nice thing to do for somebody, it's going to be fun for me to make, I'm going to have the best time ever sewing it, he's going to be happy that he's got it and no cash involved." She smiles. "It's special, it's just for him."

Amanda has been sewing ever since she can remember. With help from her mom, she began by sewing from patterns. Now she creates her own designs. When she is on tour, her mom likes Amanda to take pictures of her creations.

"I like to show her," Amanda says. "She gave me her sewing machine from when she was a youngin'. A 1966 Singer. She redid it and got all new gears so it will work just like it's brand-new. She got that ready for me for whenever I left and gave me lots of fabric and patchwork and pins and needles and thread and everything that I can do it with."

Amanda has been going on Phish and Grateful Dead tours for the last three years. In that time she has taken part in both scenes and the communities they support.

"The first Lot I ever went to was probably two or three years ago," she explains. "It was the craziest thing I had ever seen in my life, but it was also the coolest thing I'd ever seen because of the whole vibe there. That was the first time I'd ever been exposed to any serious hippiedom at all. I just heard my parents talk and they always hated it, saying that they're just filthy, dirty people that don't take care of themselves. And then when you get there, it's like, that's not what it's all about. They're much more spiritual than people ever give them credit for.

"I think my favorite, favorite part of it is like what we saw today. When that guy was like 'Hey, can you make me this?' Something so simple as that. It's just the coolest thing how everything is so homey and it's so family.

"When you really listen, besides the actual music, the words, they have the neatest stories to tell. And some of them are nice, and some of them aren't nice, but it's all just about liv-

Amanda and Samborini
(Patchwork Hats).
Photo: E. Zipern

161

ing. Period. Sort of like carpe diem. So clichéed but I think that's what a lot of the Dead has to do with. It's just like, fuck everything else, the only reason why we're here is to be happy and to take care of ourselves and each other.

"So many people, they aren't conscious of other people, they're just so self-absorbed they don't realize that there's a little bit more out there than just how many things you can put in your pocket and how many things that you can hold on to, because it doesn't matter. Even if my van dies, this kitchen caught on fire, I had no fabric, I've always got my home. I always have somewhere to go. There's not really an 'in' to it.

"One thing I really like about the Lots and the Lot scene is that somebody can have zero dollars and zero cents here. But in your average everyday scene of life, they would be on welfare and drain the welfare system for years and years. Somebody can be at zero dollars and zero cents here and get picked up and back on their feet the next day, and it's easy as saying, 'Hey, man, can you help me make a little cash?' That just totally blows my mind, and for so many people, for some reason, it has to be more complicated than this. The answer can be as simple as knocking on your neighbor's door and saying, 'Can I borrow a cup of sugar, so tomorrow I'll bring you back two cups whenever I go to the store?'

"People forget that life carries magic. It's alive and it has magic in it because there really is no explanation as to what makes something alive as opposed to not being alive. The best way to take care of yourself is to take care of somebody else. I can't think of a better way to do it."

Patchwork Ḥats
Makes 1 hat

"All the hats anybody makes, you don't necessarily make them with one person in mind, but there will always be one person that will absolutely die for that particular thing," says Amanda. "It will just jump out at you. So they're all made with lots of love and this, that, and the other thing.

"Everybody who has ever made a hat will do repairs on them," she says. "You can just start over again and strengthen one area if it's not strong enough. It's just however you want to do it, however you want it to look when you get done."

6 pieces of fabric, each cut in the shape of a triangle   A needle
Thread   Scissors

1. The way you make your hat can be very flexible. It can be as large or as small as you want depending on the number of pieces of fabric used and their size. You can use 5, 7 or more pieces, but first try using 6. "It can fluctuate," Amanda explains. "It just depends on how big and floppy you want to make the hat." Cut the fabric into 6 triangle shaped pieces. (Visualize 6 pieces in a pie). The idea is to sew these pieces together into a hat. (Diagram A)

2. Sew right sides together. The best way to do this is to sew two of the triangles together (right sides), and then set them aside. Do this three times until you have three sets of triangles that have one side sewn with another. This will enable you to line up the sides and position the colors exactly the way you want them. By doing this, you'll also be able to tell how the pieces will fit together. (Diagram B)

3. Now, piece the sides together. Working from the inside out (backward), sew right sides together again. Keep working with the pieces until they match up. (Diagram C)

   "Don't even act like you're making a hat at this point," says Amanda. "All you know you're doing is matching sides together." Sew them as sturdily as possible. When you're done, the triangles will meet.

4. Lining—You can line them, but Amanda recommends against it. When repairs need to be made (and they always will), it will be harder to see the stitches if the fabric lining is in the way.

5. Hat rim—"Cut a piece off fabric to wrap around the whole thing," she says. "That way, whenever it folds down the other way, there will be a clean edge. When it's done, sew right sides together all the way around."

6. To make the rim, you have two options. If you want your hat big and poofy, measure a piece of fabric about 35 inches long. Then, place elastic inside the fabric and fold the fabric over. According to Amanda, once the hat is adjusted to your head, it ends up being about 23 inches long. If you would prefer a fitted hat, cut a piece of fabric to the size of your head and sew that on. Either way, pleat the edge of the hat to fit the rim. (Diagram D)

7. Reinforce the stitching to keep it strong. "Reinforcement is never a bad thing when you're hand sewing," she says. "You can never have something too sturdy."

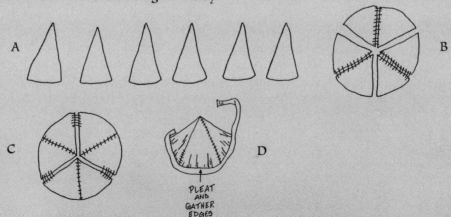

A

B

C

D

PLEAT
AND
GATHER
EDGES

Summer days in Washington, D.C. are famous for their overwhelming humidity. Evenings, too, can be unbearable, the kind where at 11 P.M., the air is still so thick with moisture, you feel like you've been swimming.

This sort of moist heat invariably seems to accompany the midsummer Dead shows at D.C.'s RFK, only interrupted by torrential episodes of warm, sticky summer rain. The downpour almost always creates a bath of mud in the part-grass, part-dirt parking lots that surround the stadium.

Fortunately, this sort of weather is perfect for the terrariums at Terrarium Station. Nicole and Kevin, terrarium makers extraordinaire, like to collect rocks, ferns, mosses and various plants that love humidity. With these materials they create striking miniature environments inside large glass bottles and jugs.

After four months of constant collecting, Nicole and Kevin's kitchen began to look like an overcrowded greenhouse, so they brought a dozen terrariums along with them to the RFK shows. Throughout the day the bottles sat in the back of Nicole and Kevin's car, out of the sun and on display.

"The only reason we're selling them is because we have so many in our kitchen." Nicole laughs. "We've been making them and then giving them away."

"And we wanted an excuse to come out here," adds Kevin.

"But the problem is, a number of people have been interested and have said, 'I'll catch up with you in Detroit, or I'll catch up with you in Missouri,' because that's where their home is," she adds. "They get on the road in a car with bad shocks, and the plants will get stressed and die."

The two began making terrariums after reading a home gardening book that featured terrarium instructions. Reading the book gave them the motivation to begin creating plant worlds inside glass.

"It was just a houseplant book, and it had a short section on terrariums, really basic," explains Nicole. "It's cool, because we've gotten books from the library and bookstores that are really detailed and more sophisticated, but I think if I had seen one of those to begin with, I would have been a lot more hesitant to start, and this made it seem so simple.

"We live in an apartment and we don't have a yard, so it's a way that we can get a little bit of nature inside. And we don't have a television so we have lots of time to devote to creative hobbies," says Kevin.

Nicole and Kevin (Terrarium Station).
Photo: E. Zipern

164

"And it's therapeutic," adds Nicole. "To come home and re-create a little natural scene for our house is very therapeutic."

When assembling their plant worlds, the couples' emphasis is on using post-consumer products or found objects. In wooded areas, they forage for plants and rocks and they also collect bottles from restaurants and recycling areas. The tools they use to position the plants within the glass are all found in the garbage, on the ground or wherever they can find them. Nicole and Kevin also like to make the terrariums with materials that are close to the heart.

"The coolest thing we did, was my grandparents used to live in Pennsylvania, and we went up there and gathered ferns and lichens and mosses and little pieces of wood, and those are some of the most beautiful ones," says Nicole. "I made one for my sister, one for my mom and one for us to keep. It's all with plants from our grandparents' land in Pennsylvania. It gives us all a little piece of our childhood to look at and stir memories."

Terrarium Station

Terrariums, also known as bottle gardens, are wonderful to make, but will take a little time and commitment to keep the foliage alive and to jury-rig the right materials. All you'll need is stuff found around the house, on the street or in the garbage. Bottles can be picked up from restaurants, recycling centers and the like. Forage for rocks and mosses in humid areas. The terra-cotta pieces can come from plant centers or a greenhouse. Also, buying the soil and the plants from a greenhouse is your best bet.

"Just mess around," say Nicole and Kevin. "Even start with one little plant and a rock. Our first one was hideous looking, but we loved it, we adored it. We looked at it a month later after we made a lot more, we were like, 'Oh God.' We actually remade it because at that time we weren't using mosses, and mosses look great!"

THOUGHTS AND TIPS FROM NICOLE AND KEVIN

*Because they're so low-maintenance, terrariums are great for kids and people who don't have good luck with plants.

*Terrariums don't do well in direct sun. The interior can get hot because the glass works like an oven and that will wilt the plants.

*Making terrariums can be very low-budget. For instance, to make the funnel, just take newspaper, wrap it up and dump the soil in.

* "Anytime anyone gazes upon nature in their house, I think it's good for their soul," says Nicole.

* "You just get so familiar with the tools," Kevin says. "We use this little hook on the end of a hanger so we can go in there and fish out stuff. It's a learn-as-you-go process."

YOU WILL NEED:

- Bottle, jar or jug—Apple cider jugs are really easy to use and perfect when just starting out. The 1-gallon organic apple juice jugs sold in many co-ops and health food stores are the perfect size. Anything will work, as long as they're about 1 to 2 gallons, have a wide mouth and short neck so that you get a lot of movement inside. Also, use clear glass, as colored glass keeps out too much light.
- Terra-cotta—Make sure the broken terra-cotta is small enough to drop through the hole of the jug but large enough to allow pockets of air between pieces. If not, break them further so that they will fit. Try calling a plant store or greenhouse to get their broken terra-cotta for free.
- Funnel—Make a funnel to fit the glass you use. "We just use a magazine," says Nicole. "We don't like to use plastic. All of our tools are pretty much post-consumer waste except that the soil came in a plastic bag."
- Soil—Buy a high-grade potting soil. Nicole and Kevin point out that this works best in keeping fungus out. Also, a large bag of soil can usually be found for under five dollars.
- Dowel—Use a dowel or thick stick to create holes in the dirt to root the plants.
- Tamper—Take a wire hanger, break off one end and pierce into a cork. Make sure the cork is sturdy and it's not going to crumble or fall off.
- Plants—Buy the plants and forage for all the mosses. Kevin and Nicole say that when foraging for moss, never remove all of a section. Take a little from here and there. This provides a diversity of mosses that is very attractive and allows the wild mosses to regenerate.

ON PLANTS. . .

"Buy plants that like a lot of humidity. You don't find many of those sitting by the side of the road. We tried it with plants we got from the park, but they didn't do very well," Nicole says.

"And if they die, they'll die pretty quickly," adds Kevin. "If they root, they'll keep growing. We had a number that didn't do well. It was touch-and-go with which plants would work. We found that some ferns and the mosses and ivy do really well. The key is to get a balance of plants so that they will grow together."

"And height makes a difference too," says Nicole. "We've brought plants home and realized they were too tall. You only have about five inches once you get all the soil in there. And the leaves that touch the side of the bottle tend to rot. There are a few exceptions, but for the most part, you don't want leaves touching the sides, it won't kill the plant, but if you can avoid it, do."

DIRECTIONS

1. Clean the bottle well and then through the funnel you've made, put in about an inch of the terra-cotta as a base. On top of that, add an inch of soil. After you have an inch, tamp it down with your tamper so it is compacted. Then add another inch and compact it down firmly so the plants have support. Landscape a slope, valley, etc., by making levels with the dirt.

→

2. Before beginning to add plants, figure out the arrangement or scene that you want to create. "Our book suggests that you draw it out," says Nicole. "We really haven't done that, just in our head. If you try to make it look like a landscape, we found that that works best. You would be amazed at these little plants, the way you can find little ones that look like trees and little elder greens. One of the suggestions that we saw in one of the more sophisticated books is that you try to imagine a landscape and then recreate it."

3. Use a dowel to create holes in the dirt for the plants. (Diagram A) In their alley, Kevin and Nicole found wood that was thin enough to go in the jar but still large enough to make a hole in the dirt. Make the hole and then gently lower the plants in. Make sure all the leaves are up. "You have to be gentle with the plants at all times," says Nicole. "Take the plants and remove the soil from the roots." Nicole and Kevin run the roots under water to clean the soil off. From here they say it's a manipulation game of getting the plants rooted. Make sure all the roots are firmly anchored as you scrape the dirt back into the hole and around the plant. Then use the cork to tamp the soil down. Be gentle with the stick! To fit the moss in the hole, break it up so each piece is no larger than a quarter. Then, push down firmly with the cork to get it to take hold, because moss needs a firm foundation.

4. Arrangements—Use pebbles, sticks, rocks, stones and crystals to make a landscape.

5. Once the planting process is complete, the glass will inevitably be covered in soil, so take a moist natural sponge, tie it around something long, (like a section of hanger wire) and clear the dirt from the inside of the glass. Then wipe down the outside.

6. Water—Usually the soil is moist when you put it in and if you use moss, that will sometimes be damp too. Kevin and Nicole don't water their terrariums when they begin. "The quickest way to kill a terrarium is with too much water," says Kevin. "If you have a calendar and you can make yourself do it, mark and water it with *one teaspoon* once a month." The jug opening is so small that very little water is lost to evaporation.

7. Upkeep. The plants will continue growing in the terrarium, so check often to see if any of them need pruning. Do this by attaching a sharp knife or scalpel to a dowel. Remove any rotten leaves on the plants to prevent disease from spreading and use the sponge to wipe away any mildew (a sign of over-watering). Keep in bright, *indirect* sunlight and water once a month. (Diagram B)

A

B

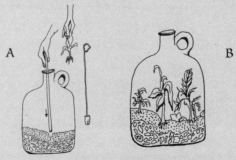

Ever since they adapted a nineteenth-century illustration depicting a wiry skeleton with roses encircling its head as one of their emblems, some of the Grateful Dead's larger than life symbols have involved roses. Meshing particularly well with the sixties generation of flower power, much of the art surrounding the Grateful Dead has involved the thorny blossom, as have many of the song lyrics.

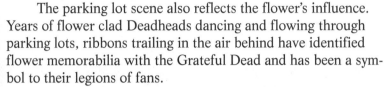

Allen and Mark (Flower Wreaths).
Photo: E. Zipern

The parking lot scene also reflects the flower's influence. Years of flower clad Deadheads dancing and flowing through parking lots, ribbons trailing in the air behind have identified flower memorabilia with the Grateful Dead and has been a symbol to their legions of fans.

Allen is especially adept at weaving individual flowers into beautiful wreathes and hair adornments. When his friend Mark suggested they travel from Virginia to the 1995 RFK shows, the two made the trip, bringing buckets of fresh flowers along with them.

"I've been working with plants for the last ten years, wreaths for the last five years, off and on," remarks Allen. "I just picked up some flowers, had been doing fresh flower work for a while, and it was just a natural transition to go to.

"I like working with flowers because of the color differences, the petal shapes and the different ways they express themselves. Obviously they go back to the flower power days, but everything has always flowed with them in a special way. Flowers represent that life-and-death kind of issue. The relationship of the flower to the reproductive nature. The one major reason that keeps me attracted to flowers is the healing quality that each flower transmits.

"Flowers are an expression of going beyond into a more spiritual space. It's the plant letting go of the seeds, a spiritual experience. I guess that's how life is."

Flower Wreaths

"It takes about forty-five minutes to one hour to make them," says Allen. "It's relaxing, especially if you have all your materials around and you don't have to get up and down. It can be very meditative and addicting, like anything else. It can get quite complicated and weird in your mind when you work with these things.

"Unless you're living in an urban setting, go for a walk and look around at what's blooming. Start picking one or two different flowers, and you'll end up with what you need. Also, think in terms of what it's going to look like when it's dry."

Allen says that herbs possess healing properties when they are around you. "With wreathes it is using them mainly as mandalas. . . to hold an energy pattern, thought or idea."

Florist wire—22 gauge. A very thin, green wire, this inexpensive material can be found at most any florist shop. Call around to find some.

Flowers—Allen recommends using sage, thyme, rosemary, yarrow, vines and grasses. "Black-eyed Susans will dry well and get rustic. They don't hold their form too well, but the color is nice."

1. You can create your wreath by using only one type of flower, or mix it up with a variety. (Allen suggests weaving with different flowers.) First, take a sturdy flower that has a long and very flexible stem (like yarrow which bends easily) and use it as a base. The idea is to lay the flower heads against each other, continually adding and tying on until a thick garland of flowers is created. So, begin by placing another flower head under the first. (The other flower stems can be short.) Then, secure each flower by tying with florist wire. (Diagram A)

2. Continue adding and tying until you have a long garland. To transform into a wreath, just wrap the ends together into a circle and secure. (Diagram B) If one area looks bare or needs more flowers, add them in. Additional flowers can be added throughout.

3. Now, let your wreath dry. "When it dries, it will dry into quite a little system, it will be a memorialization, something for the altar," says Allen. "If some of the flowers fall apart, yank them from the arrangement."

A   B

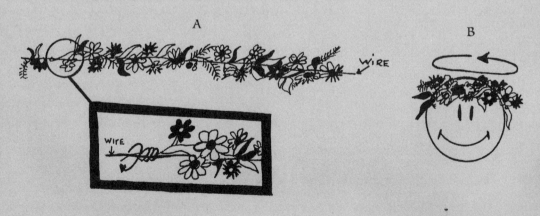

On Soldier Field's blacktop paved parking lot, Phil, Dave and Mike sit around a fuzzy orange and yellow blanket which lies in front of their car. Surrounding them are coolers full of icy cold drinks, food to munch on and a set of Devil Sticks they assembled before the annual Chicago shows. A few years back, the three began to dabble in making Devil Sticks after a long period of playing with them.

"We just started to try to make a pair and the first couple came out really bad, but we eventually found what we liked and we sold them at school," says Mike. "They used to sell real well, but these days, the market is getting flooded."

In recent years, the tremendous popularity of Grateful Dead shows has spotlighted unusual crafts sometimes unfamiliar to the mainstream public. Devil Sticks, hacky sacks and juggling are customary Lot activities which can quickly entrance those who play with them. The trick and the addiction to Devil Sticks has to do with balance. Using two hand sticks, the key is to balance a larger stick by spinning it back and forth, around, and into the air.

"Someone at a show last year told me that it's a form of meditation somewhere in Africa," says Dave. "When you get really involved in them, it's all you think about. Actually, you don't even think about it once you get the hang of it, you just don't think."

"They're addictive," adds Phil. "Once you start playing them, you can't stop. I can sit there for hours and just jam out. Especially when you're learning, you're always learning more things everyday and it keeps you wanting to learn more.

"I remember when I first grabbed them, I couldn't even balance one, but now, it's just so simple," he continues. "You don't even think about it, you just do it. It takes a month of dedication, that's what I've been telling people. A month of hard work and you'll be good, and you'll just love it because it'll be so much fun. The first month, it's so hard. I remember I kept dropping them. I'd be up at night, twelve-thirty in the morning playing with them. I just stuck with it."

Dave, Phil and Mike (Devil Sticks). Photo: E. Zipern

Devil Sticks
Makes 1 pair

Balance is extremely important when making Devil Sticks. The same is true for spinning them. Phil, Mike and Dave say it's all about practice. The general idea is to spin the main stick between the two hand sticks by keeping the weight even. The shape and size of the sticks influences the way they will spin.

YOU'LL NEED:

Dowel rods all the same length, 16 to 18 inches long

Rubber splicing tape

Colored electrical tape (use two or three different colors to make great designs!)

Backed vinyl, cut

Tape measure

This is a three-part instruction

THE LARGER SPINNING STICK

1. Cut (or buy) a dowel rod about 16 to 18 inches long and 5/8 of an inch thick. (Diagram A)
2. Take rubber splicing tape and wrap the entire dowel, overlapping halfway over the previous wrap each time you wrap around. (Diagram B) In order for it to turn well, the stick needs to be heavier on the ends, so attach a vinyl fringe to both ends. (Ideally, a special saw to carve the rod in this shape would provide the right balance.)
3. Cut backed vinyl to create a fringe. (Do this twice to make a piece for both ends.) Cut the vinyl about 4 inches long and 10-15 inches wide (longer width equals more weight—Mike uses about 12-15 inches). Into the length, make 6 cuts, each 1 to 2 inches long. (Diagram C) This will appear frayed once the stick's ends are wrapped.
4. Wrap the fringe around the ends and secure with colored electrical tape. (Diagram D) Squeeze tight. "It won't be really tight, so wrap like hell," they say. Wrap and decorate with the colored tape. If you use three different colors, you can create designs and layers of color.

TWO HAND STICKS

These sticks will be thinner and lighter than the larger, spinning stick. Do the following process twice to create two hand sticks.

1. Cut the dowel rods 16 to 18 inches long and 3/8 inches in width. Wrap in the same manner as the main stick. But, unlike the main one, these should be evenly wrapped.

↓

2. Once wrapped, keep the sticks apart for a while. Sometimes they stick together when they're first wrapped. If they do stick, don't pull, gently roll apart.

3. On one end of the hand sticks, Mike, Dave and Phil wrap extra tape to create handgrips. On the other end, they sometimes wrap an extra 6 inches of tape to better grip the larger stick as it spins.

Now you should have a wonderful set of Devil Sticks! (Diagram E)

HOW TO PLAY WITH DEVIL STICKS
Practice is the teacher on this one. But start off with the main stick standing upright on the ground and tap back and forth with the hand sticks to get the flow of how they work. Eventually, begin to lift the stick off the ground, spinning and juggling it with the hand sticks.

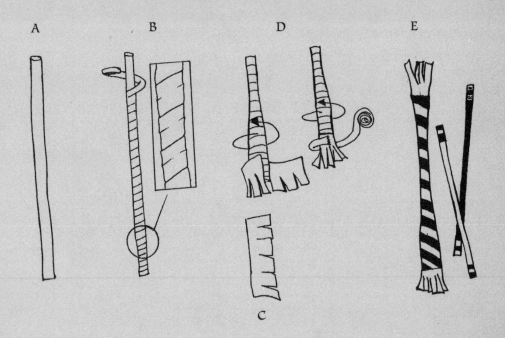

A   B   D   E

C

It is 11:30 in the morning. Miles of cars, trucks, buses, vans and the occasional local television crew crawl by at a snail's pace. Already sitting for hours, anxious and perhaps bored, passengers sit on roofs, hoods and trunks, laughing, listening to music and watching the circus as it slowly moves on.

The road is Route 78. It is a small, two-lane thoroughfare in northwestern Vermont that runs through the towns of Highgate, East Highgate and down the street to the Franklin County airport. Usually quiet, the June 15 Grateful Dead show scheduled at the airport transformed the roadway into a virtual parking lot for thousands of colorful, sticker covered vehicles making their way to see the show.

As the day unfolded, the sides along the roadway are transformed into a long, wide Shakedown which stretched between the makeshift campgrounds which residents leased out their yards for, and the entrance to the airport. Vehicular and pedestrian congestion was inevitable. Weaving in and out of the cars, people were everywhere, walking in every direction, attempting to make their way up and down the crowded, improvised Shakedown.

With so many people walking by, Normandie laid out a shiny, rose-colored, metallic square of fabric to accentuate the hemp jewelry, embroidered hats and hand designed organic cotton T-shirts she brought to vend. Selling her creations will help her pay for tickets as well as buy more hemp twine and fabric to make future jewelry, hats and pouches.

In the years since she has been going to Grateful Dead shows, Normandie has dedicated a great deal of time at home and on the road creating crafts that would pay for her continually intrepid habit of traveling. She remembers her first Grateful Dead experiences.

Normandie (Embroidery).
Photo: Mark Dabelstein

"My first show felt really comfortable," says Normandie. "It was kinda what I had expected. I had hung out with people who had gone to shows for a while. I just remember feeling really happy and content inside that show. From the beginning I was fascinated by the whole world of it.

"That first show and my experience of being in the scene was the hook and ever since then

173

I've been drawn more and more to it. I hadn't been hit by the music yet, but I was definitely intrigued by the whole thing and knew that it was something that I wanted to get more of.

"I can pinpoint the show where the music hit me, which was actually a couple of years later. They played really great, there was this amazing energy. It was at the Cap Center in the spring of 1990. It was the first of three shows, and some people that I was with had been going a lot more than me. I remember coming out of the show and being like, 'Okay, I understand now!'" She remembers. "I really felt the power and the energy of the music that night, just being swept away and feeling that joy. I remember thinking at that point, 'Now I'm a Deadhead. Uh-oh, this is a habit now!'"

Normandie fell in love with the music, but felt hesitant to drop everything to go on tour. Over time, she noticed a steady progression of becoming more involved in going to shows, until she found herself doing full tours.

"The more I was around it, the more I fell in love with it, all the way even through this past summer," she explains. "But I hesitated from the very start. Should I just drop everything and hop on tour? I always have this feeling in my head that I need to be going and saving the world. I need to be doing my work and not just running around, playing with the Grateful Dead, as much as I love it. I think there was this voice in the back of my head, saying, 'Normandie, you have to get on with your life.' And now it's kind of funny, because when I look back on the last couple years of my life, all I really was doing was either going on tour or getting ready to go on tour or trying to recover from tour or dreaming about being at shows."

"Something that's grown on me more and more over the years, is what the songs are about and the words to the songs. They're little messages to me about different things in my life. And so many nights there's that song, even though you've heard it a million times, that hits you in some new and powerful way. It speaks directly to what's happening in your life. Over time it became apparent to me that everybody loves what they sing about because it's all about traveling and how we live. The music itself, Jerry's guitar playing, the notes, the way they come out of his guitar. It's just really, really beautiful, touching, a way that I've never heard anybody else play a guitar. And the improvisation. The music has such a life and energy of its own.

"Music is such a channel to higher things, and dancing. The boys in the band know that, and they create an atmosphere for that to be, a place where people can experience that. There's also a precedence for it there. People go, expecting this to be a religious experience, so it is. It's a safe place for that to happen. It's partly coming from the band but also coming from the energy of the audience who are using it as a place for spiritual awakening, and therapy and revelation.

"I believe that as human beings, we have a need to join ourselves with some higher force, through music and dancing. Unfortunately, in Western society, that's not something that is accepted, encouraged or thought to be important. Luckily, here and there have been people who have figured out places where they can fill that need, and the Grateful Dead has been one of those places. It's a need that every human being has and filling that makes us fuller and better and happier people, so that we can go forth into the world and make it a better place. If you're a happier and more fulfilled person, you can't help but improve our world."

Embroidery

A THOUGHT FROM NORMANDIE AS YOU SEW...
"There is this awesome quote I saw on my brother's wall the other day. It says, 'Work as if money doesn't mean anything, dance as if no one's watching, and love as if you'll never be hurt.' I thought that was really cool."

WHAT YOU'LL NEED:
Fabric—"It definitely works better on a heavier piece of fabric, like corduroy."
Embroidery floss—This can be found at the fabric or craft store, in a variety of colors.
Needle—Normandie tries to use a needle with a small eye but finds it more difficult to thread.
Scissors—They don't need to be fancy, but sharp scissors will cut the floss neater so that it is easier to thread.

TIPS...
* *Things to embroider on to—Patches and different clothing. "Do it somewhere you're going to be able to see it a lot," says Normandie. "It's really neat to use embroidery along the edges of pockets, just as little decorations here or there, on your clothes, on your hat."*
* *Things that are easy to embroider—Flowers! "I do a lot of flowery sort of things, floral, viney things are easy, I also like to do stars," she says. "I would suggest trying some abstract designs, maybe just different patterns of colors. Be creative with what you do and don't be restricted by things you've actually seen."*
* *"Anything I've ever done, I kinda just played with. I start my pieces with an idea in mind, but it always changes. Some people like to draw it out on the fabric first and follow the lines they're drawn. No one way is right or wrong, it's just whatever you like the most."*

↓

* "Someone gave me an embroidery hoop. It helps to keep the fabric taut, and it makes it so when you're pulling the stitches through, they stay nice and flat and even. It can be helpful. The one I have is a little circle."
* "What really affects the wear and tear on all your clothing, including things that are embroidered, is the way you wash and dry them. I always tell people to wash their stuff in a really mild detergent and don't put your clothes in the dryer. *Especially if you're sick of patching them all the time. Your clothes will last a lot longer, and our earth will be a lot happier."*

STITCHES

There are many variations on the stitches you can use. Some are: the back stitch, basic running stitch, chain stitch (and variations on this) and the patch stitch. To make things easier, only the basic, running and patch stitch are included here. Whichever stitch you use, begin by tying a double knot in the end of the floss and pull up from the bottom of the fabric.

• Basic Stitch—This is a very common stitch. It is done wherever needed or in designs like circles (Diagram A), next to each other (Diagram B) or wherever (Diagram C).

• Running Stitch—This stitch is a quick and easy way to create a line. Simply stitch up and down in a row. (Diagram D)

• Patch Stitch

1. Start by bringing the thread through the back piece of fabric, directly next to the patch. (Diagram E)
2. Take the needle through the patch a bit in from the edge, and a little to the right of the first stitch. (Diagram F)
3. Come up through next to the patch again and then *through* the loop of the first stitch. (Diagram G)
4. Pull the first stitch tight and make the next stitch to the right of the first. (Diagram H)
5. Continue to repeat steps 3 and 4 all the way around the patch. (Diagram I)

*Patching Notes
—Make sure the patch is big enough to cover the hole and the worn area around it.
—Use medium-heavy fabric.
—Normandie says this is an important skill for all conscious earth-residents!

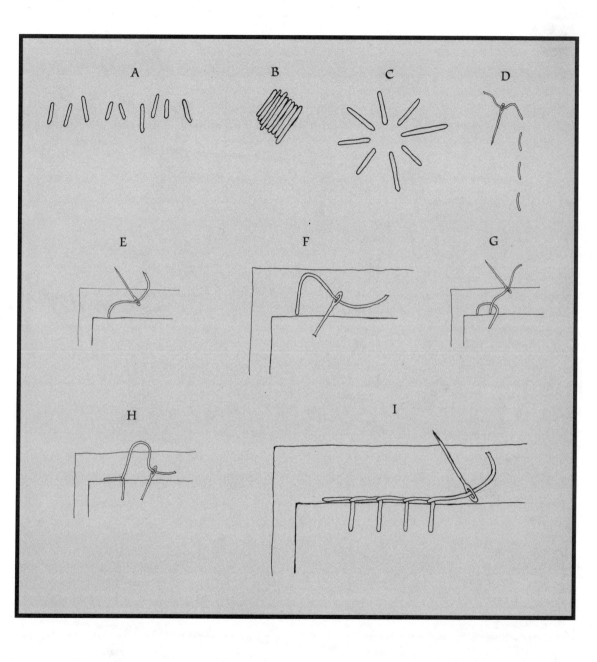

✿ Assorted Thoughts. . . ✿

A favorite musical entree, courtesy of William Patton. Here's how you can enjoy this tasty feast. . .

"You will need:
—a CD player which can play at least 3 CD's successively
—about 3 hours to kill

Simply add these ingredients (in the order listed):
—Any Bob Marley album (I find 'Uprising' to be particularly flavorful)
—one big, thick terrapin (the whole thing), marinated in Donna sauce
—a helping of 'Floyd's' Atom Heart Mother (might not be in your cupboard, but it's worth bor-
    rowing a cup from your neighbor);
Delicious, nutritious and prepared in just minutes. It has a crunchy reggae consistency and
    leaves a cheesy Gothic aftertaste, but it's very, very sweet at the center. Best served slightly
    louder than room temperature with some *kind* garnishings."

GRATEFUL FOOD FOR THOUGHT. . .
BY JOLIE GOODMAN AND ARDAS KHALSA

The Promised Ham
Tennessee Headcheese
Snacks of My Life
Picasso Spoon
Ala-Jama-Getaway
Nobody's Malt But Mine
The Other Won Ton
Scarlet Bialys
Black Mud Pie
New Spaghetti Boogie

Black-Coated Ribs
Morning Brew
It's All Over Now, Baby Blueberry
Me and My Onions
Victim or the Lime
Let the Good Pies Roll
Two Colas in Communion
King Pea
Tons of Veal
Fire in the Salsa

Throwing Bones
Big River of Gravy
Cold Rain and Snow Cones
Deep Jell-O Blues
Jack Strawberry Waffle
Ripple Potato Chips

Wharf Ratatouille
Box of Grains
Saint Steamers
Dark Toast
Too Sugaree
Eyes of the Potato

Lime Tart: Lemon Tarter
Pies of the World
Estimated Crop Yield
What's Become of the Baby
   Peas and Carrots?
The Golden Road to
   Unlimited Chocolate

MORE. . .
BY JOHN E. DVORAK

Cucumberland Blues
Don't Grease Me In
Fries of the World
I Need a Popsicle
Grillin' on Heaven's Door
Little Dead Rooster
Mama Fried

Stella Blue Cheese
Touch of Grey Poupon
Wang Dang Cheese
   Doodles
Weather Report Sweets
Ground (and) Round
Hell in a Bucket of KFC
Jack-A-Fish-Egg

Cheese Gone
China Cat Sunflower Seeds
Crazy Chicken Fingers
New French Fried Potato
   Caboose
Shake and Bakedown Street
Batter Lee
I Bought the Slaw

Flecks of glitter
gum
and spilt beer
take up the floor
assuming their positions on our feet
sticking, gripping
moist, sweaty dirt all over us. . .
feet wrapped tightly in desire and passion
and spinning
THIS is pleasure. . .
How does it end in these rotations?
                    -E. ZIPERN

The Author in Chicago (Last Show).
Photo: Mark Dabelstein

179

Photo: Alec Bauer

✿ Jerry Garcia... ✿

ASHLEY ALDERMAN
CONGO BARS
   Jerry's passing is very sad to me. But I now appreciate the experiences I have had at Dead shows even more. I will always cherish having gone. Now I will cherish the music for what it stands for. Jerry's spirit will live on forever, through his music, and through the subculture he helped create. What a beautiful contribution.

JEFF KAY
DANK BRAN AND BOOTYLICIOUS BLUEBERRY MUFFINS
   To say that the death of Jerry Garcia is the end of an era is an understatement. It will likely lead to the end of a culture, which for thirty years, has existed under the surface of American society. Though the Dead had been playing for over ten years before I was born, I will be forever grateful for having had the opportunity to be a Deadhead for a few years.

ERIC KABIK
ERIC'S FANTASTIC VEGGIE RICE BURRITO
   I feel like I have lost a very close family member, as I have in an abstract way. Jerry was not the Grateful Dead but at the core of the experience, his essence was essential. Was. . . it feels weird to say

181

that. I will miss him greatly, but feel blessed to have been around to share so much with him. I hope his music is carried out through generations as a symbol of what a humble, intelligent, sincere man can accomplish through music. Much love to all of my brothers, sisters and Dead family—without love in the dream, it'll never come true. . . . Keep it alive!

DONYELE
VEGAN TACO SALAD

I haven't experienced the kind of joy and ecstasy I've felt at Dead shows anywhere else in my life. I get really sad when I think about that, and I truly hope that I find something else as wonderful as a Dead show. Someone once described a show to me as thousands of people, all making love to each other at the same time. That seems about right. I absolutely loved being at a show and dancing with a group of people, giving them energy and getting energy from them. Then Jerry would forget the words or sing something especially beautiful or play something extraordinary on his guitar and you would look at each other, you and these people you don't know, strangers stopping strangers, just to shake their hand, and you would smile, you would beam and glow. Joyous.

GREG JOHNSON
HOMEMADE VEGGIE SOUP

Jerry,

Your passing opens a hole inside my heart that cannot be filled. I must admit that I was selfish about it, at first. "What will I do now? I wanted my kids to share the Dead with me." Thoughts like that. But now it goes way beyond me and I have empathy for your family and friends.

A lot of folks don't understand how someone I never met or would never meet could affect me so. They never will understand how you, your music and all that surrounded you became a part of me, as vital as the blood that pumps through me. I wish you could have gotten clean, but no matter what anyone believes about death, your suffering has ended. It has a sort of ironic joy to it. I still cry about this, but many times I find myself smiling. Thank you for twenty years, over one hundred shows and both the best and worst memories of my life. I shared some of the most profound and life-shaping experiences with you guys and would never trade that for anything. I will never listen to another bootleg without that sad, happy, smile on my face.

> Rest in Peace
> I love you
> Greg

NICOLE
TERRARIUM STATION

We mourned Jerry's departure from this earth as we would a beloved brother and friend. But he has left us with a glorious legacy of music and memories. Though I would have wished for him the wonders of a long life and old age, Jerry's time was enough to brighten the lives of millions. That is a rare and cherished accomplishment.

KEVIN
TERRARIUM STATION

As a bike courier in D.C., I spent a lot of time peddling my bike and listening to the Dead on my headphones. Every day Jerry would brighten the rainiest of days. One day as I listened to "Scarlet Begonias" (and singing along, of course) I stopped to use a pay phone to call my dispatcher. When I got off the phone, I caught the eye of the young man waiting behind me. Maybe it was the Dead sticker on my bike, or him hearing me sing along with Jerry that made him say hello. He, too, loved Jerry and we proceeded to talk for twenty minutes. We parted feeling good about ourselves as we shook each other's hands and said good-bye. Strangers stopping strangers just to shake their hand. I think Jerry would have liked our little interlude.

Thanks, Jerry
Kevin

MIKE SOOP
DEVIL STICKS

The Dead represent that community where everyone can be free. To share, to experience, "to love and learn and grow." It's definitely a tragedy losing him. He was our spiritual guide on this journey called life. Though few actually met Jerry, everyone feels like they knew him. The Dead have suffered other losses, and the band kept playin' on, though this may prove to be the most painful. But as long as our brothers and sisters keep the memories and the tape trading alive, the music will never stop.

Keep Dancing,
Mike

PHIL
DEVIL STICKS

Jerry had so much to offer, even if you don't like rock music, hell, even music. Jerry should be remembered as an innovator as much as Picasso.

Thanx, Jer
Phil

MER
SALVE AND MASSAGE OIL

We were shot into the stratosphere, danced and howled and went crazy, and then came back to warm hugs and big smiles. And the music made us do it.

Live passionately, my friends.

NORMANDIE HYATT
EMBROIDERY

There's something that we feel, that our family feels, when the music starts playing and you start skipping around in circles and there's just that smile on your face that won't go away, and everybody is there together. I'm going to miss that excitement of running in, holding that miracle ticket, when you're just floating above the ground. A sense of being at home.

183

One thing that came into my head, was of wanting to thank people. Thank everyone all along the road that has touched me and been a part of our experience together. It has meant so much to me in my life. I want to encourage people to take all the joy and happiness they received through their lives with the Grateful Dead, and go onward and spread it to everyone else. Always remember the power of music and that there is much more magic we're going to run into that we haven't even dreamt of. If we just believe it's going to happen, it can be just as special as the Grateful Dead has been.

STEPHANIE
CHEF STEF'S CHICKPEA CHAPATIS

The outpouring of grief over Jerry's passage, and celebration for his gift of music for the world has been overwhelming, and a comfort to those who will really miss him. He touched an incredible number of people, from his best fans to the occasional listener, with his spirit, soul and good heart. Thanks, Jerry, for all the good times with lots o' love.

CATHERINE
ORGANIC VEGGIE ROLL UP

I really hope that I can have another opportunity to go and experience another show. It's such a peaceful, harmonious feeling that you walk away with, you feel really centered and it gives you that energy that you need to come back and deal with real life. So it's something that I will truly miss, but I'm very thankful for all that I have experienced.

ELSKA KING
ELSKA'S HAIR SCRUNCHIES

When summer flies
and August dies
and world goes dark and mean
Comes the shimmering of the
moon on black infested trees
I've loved
I've learned
I've grown
How much you'll never know!
Thank you Jerry
It's our turn now!

CORRIE COLBERT
HEMP SEED COOKIES OF JOY

I don't even know how to feel now that Jerry is gone. Just because he's gone, doesn't mean he would want us to stop getting together. Maybe it's time to look inward. There are big changes, good changes happening and I think we're all going to come together. Maybe it was a sign to start looking into ourselves, just starting new. . . I still feel numb. I'm just fortunate that I found them when I did. We have to think about Jerry too. He's reached the next realm, he's totally at the next level. I'm sure he's playing his guitar and feeling good.

LYNN
VEGAN SPRING ROLLS WITH THAI PEANUT SAUCE

So much cosmic energy surrounds the whole departure. I do not see him as gone, for now he is everywhere. In this day and age with all the negativity around us, we must start to see the light within ourselves, develop it and be that which Jerry so desperately tried to communicate to us. Take that light of self and let if flow outward. We are all one, one in energy. Time for re-evaluation of self. Jerry's time was over on this dimension, but he will live on forever, an unknown legend. Now, many say Jerry is GOD—so true yet many fail to see that each and everyone of us is GOD—all small parts of a large whole—the almighty IS! It's about BLISS—LOVE, self-worth. "Wake up to find out that you are the eyes of the world. . ." The only thing that truly keeps us apart from Jerry is our unwillingness to break down the barrier our society has created around our heightened consciousness. We all can be together, here and now, and Jerry more than anyone taught me this.

CHRIS
FAVA BEAN SALAD AND SANDWICH

Jerry,
You have shown what can happen when one follows his or her bliss. I could only imagine the world if everyone did. Thanks.

AMANDA
RICE AND VEGGIE WRAP

Jerry's death is our cue to relate what we've learned here back to those people who need it the most. We are all brothers and sisters and if we love and respect and try to understand each other, there is that much more love and respect and understanding in the world. It's in our hands now.

JASON
FAVA BEAN SALAD AND SANDWICH

*When naked ghosts of
ancient Indian*

chemicals of rhythm
come to dwell
within the cavity
of your chest,
to dance in
beat with the clock tick
of the Universe,
that licks the eardrums of small
wide-eyed
children
who are exploring
the intricate
design and color
in the fibers
of the carpet world;
I will be
a particle
shaking three
blue
marbles
in my hand
meeting you again
and again
in the pattern
while energy
is never
lost. . .

DAVE HAMLIN
THE ELEPHANT EAR PEOPLE

Like gold fills the leaves in the wind, long roads numberless as the wings of trees! The long years have passed like swift draughts of the sweet wine in lofty halls beyond the West, beneath the Blue skies of earth where the stars trembled in the song of his voice, holy and kingly. Who now shall fill the cup for me? For now, the kinder, queen of space has uplifted her hands like clouds and angry country darkness lies on the foaming waves. . . Farewell! Maybe you shall find peace, Jerry, Farewell! Namaste Garcia.

ALLIE
TVP WITH PASTA AND SAUCE
      And so blow the winds of change. Thank you, Jerry, for providing the music that is part of the soundtrack to my life. As to the future, Jerry's death is a blessing in disguise. So many bright shining lights—strong people equals strong force—now are set free in the world and somewhat forced to do other things. I hope with all my heart that we can focus on good and help heal our world.

PAUL
SHANGHAI NOODLES
      Jerry will be missed dearly. The amount of joy, love, music and ultimate bliss that he created for all was endless. The magic must be kept alive. In Jerry's name, let's live our lives to the way he would want us to. Live the way we learned through the music and lyrics of the Grateful Dead. We love you, Jerry.

MELANIE
THE VEGGIE SISTERS POTATO BURRITO AND SOLAR CANDLES

A silver halo framing his face
eyes intent upon his guitar,
fingers dancing,
melodies flowing,
Flying with music as wings so
very far. . .
Another place in the circle of life,
hand in hand with loved ones,
dancing and surrounding the light.
Telling stories,
Sharing songs,
Laughing together, deep into the night. . .
Gaze up to the stars and imagine
beautiful angels,
Feel your soul and remember special
places,
Listen to the music and think
of the man,
Grandfather of time, always, Playin in the Band.. . .
                              —love always,
                              Melanie Rose

CHASE ANN
TOFU POT PIE
I feel very fortunate that I was able to go on tour as long as I did. The memories will stay in my heart forever and the friendships I'll always treasure. Jerry gave all he had to us and he made my life so happy. I still feel him around us everyday. If I can shed some of the light and happiness to others that Jerry gave to me, I will be content. I am very blessed.

RICH
RICH'S VEGAN BURRITOS
I was born and raised in San Anselmo, California, where Jerry Garcia is a household name and bumping into band members is common. With vending money and odd jobs when I was home, I was able to tour for four years, missing less than twenty shows, never asking for a miracle and keeping a place to rest my bones between tour. This adventure was the best thing I've done so far in my life, and I will never forget all the memories and friends I met. I also learned a great lesson by following the example the Dead set. You only get out of life what you put into it. If everyone took care of themselves with a little left over for others, the world would be a better place. Remember that when life gets a little hard.

ELIZABETH
CAJUN FRENCH FRIES
I think I heard Bob Weir say the night Jerry died, "Papa's gone, we are on our own." It's like that, when your father dies, you carry on his legacy. I don't think the music should stop, maybe the band should stop, but the music is always going to go on. I can say for myself, it has brought together a family of people, very close friends. We live all over the country. We wouldn't be as close friends as we are if it weren't for seeing shows together. There's just a lot of us. Jerry brought us all together so often, so easily, it's going to take a lot more effort, but I think that somehow we should create a reunion of sorts. It will be a lot harder, but I think that it should happen, because it's a good thing. Jerry touched each of us in a very personal way.

✿ Acknowledgments ✿

Immeasurable gratitude is once again extended to all who participated and assisted in this second recording of the Grateful Dead parking lot world. Infinite thanks and praise to all of the vendors featured herein. Special thanks to Carla, Miranda, Lynn, Chase and Rich, everyone in the Last Supper Kitchen, Kate and Alice, Corrie and her wonderful cookies, Elska, Mike (my tie-dye friend), Normandie—omniscient creative craft consultant, the lovely Candace, and the ever-decadent Donna.

Without the visual creativity of my photographer-printer friend, Mark Dabelstein, and Raquel (Rock Out!) Heiny, nothing would be quite as clear. I am indebted to you both. Thank you for your support and as always, your friendship.

To everyone at St. Martin's Press for the opportunity of a second round at this. To my editor, Jennifer Enderlin, her assistant, Amy Kolenik, and my insightful and supportive publicist, Jessica Varner. Thanks also to Jim Trupin, and as always, Elizabeth Beier for getting this whole ball rolling in the first place.

Special thanks, appreciation and admiration to my dad and also to my mother (SPC Director extraordinaire!), especially for her tremendous input, care, ideas, editing and dedication. They have both always had faith in this project and in me.

Thanks and love to the intrepid gang, Lynne Brown, Norm and KRAM. Also to Andrew, the brother phat ass, Danielle DeCastro, Jen and Marty, Kristan Farley, Rocko, Steve, Lori, (and the Vin-man), Gregg Morris, Soraya and Elijah James, Sandy Brodie, Alec-olive-juice, Talia Rotblum, Kevin White, Carmen Spiech, The On-Line Grateful Dead Family, all the pets—Shadow, Scooter, Jake, Coal, Samantha, Kaya and Bear. And of course, thanks to the many doodes continually roaming throughout this expansive land of ours. . . Alen, Kanad, Amy, Mass, Larry, Mike, Kevin and Andre, etc. etc. (the list could be endless).

(In the last book I listed everyone who ever existed, so if further acknowledging you desire, please refer to the acknowledgment section in the front of *Cooking with the Dead* for a more complete and oh so long list.)

In the interest of space and time, let me just say. . . thank you, for I am eternally Grateful.

Keep the faith!

❀ Sources ❀

Bates, Dorothy. *The TVP Cookbook.* Tennessee: The Book Publishing Co., 1991.

Brandelius, Jerilyn Lee. *Grateful Dead Family Album.* New York: Warner Books, 1989.

Colbin, Annemarie. *The Natural Gourmet.* New York: Ballantine Books, 1989.

Jaffrey, Madhur. *Madhur Jaffrey's Indian Cooking.* New York and London: Barron's Educational
    Services, Inc. and BBC Books, 1994 (revised).

Osborne, Laura. *The Rasta Cookbook.* New Jersey: Africa World Press, 1992.

Rinzler, Carol Ann. *Herbs, Spices and Condiments.* New York: Harry Holt & Company, Inc., 1990.

Saltzman, Joanne. *Amazing Grains.* California: HJ Kramer, Inc., 1990.

Shenk, David, and Steve Silberman. *Skeleton Key—A Dictionary for Deadheads.* New York: Doubleday,
    1994.

Shulman, Martha Rose. *Fast Vegetarian Feasts.* New York: Doubleday, 1982.

Tierra, Michael. *The Way of Herbs.* New York: Pocket Books, 1980.

Whitman, Joan, and Delores Simon. *Recipes into Type.* New York: Harper Collins Publishers, 1993.

Williams, Dar. *The Tofu Tollbooth.* Massachusetts: Ardwork Press, 1994.

✿ Resources and Notes ✿

•The Ohio Hempery—The Ohio Hempery can supply most any product derived from hemp, including hemp seeds, hemp twine, fabric, clothing, paper and personal care products. They also carry the pro-hemp book, *The Emperor Wears No Clothes,* by Jack Herer. To request a catalog or ask any questions, call 1-800-BUY-HEMP or (614) 662-4367.

• The Dharma Trading Co.—To order the dye for tie-dyes. Request their free catalog or ask questions. 1-800-542-5227.

• The Tofu Tollbooth—A book absolutely essential for anyone wishing to eat well on the road. Lists all the natural food across America by state. Call 1-800-TOFU-2-GO.

• Co-op America—Publisher of the National Green Pages. This is an annual directory of socially responsible (environmentally sound) businesses. It includes numerous listings of food co-ops and food stores, but is not limited to just that. This directory can help to locate green business of all types, national and local. Call 1-800-584-7336 for more information and to receive a copy.

• The Rex Foundation—The Rex Foundation is a charitable, in-house organization set up by the Grateful Dead and supported by their annual concerts. It is named after Grateful Dead roadie, Rex Jackson, who died in an automobile accident. The Rex Foundation promotes the humanities and the arts, as well as causes such as the Haight-Ashbury Free Clinic. More information can be obtained by writing:

> The Rex Foundation
> P.O. Box 2204
> San Anselmo, CA 94979
> Tax ID #68 0033257

❀ Glossary ❀

"Let your food be your medicine, let your medicine be your food"

Following is a quick glossary of foods listed within. Many of these ingredients cannot be found in mainstream supermarkets, only in natural food stores, co-ops or international markets. Because of advertising, lives lived in the fast lane and a general lack of education, much of the United States relies on fast food or prepackaged food products. The emphasis has been drawn away from cooking, so many of the ingredients listed here are new, and understandably seem scary.

Stores that offer organic, pesticide-free products can open doorways into other worlds of culinary, spiritual and nutritional thought. Natural food centers aren't just about food. They are resources, places for people to come together as a community and learn, not just about food, but about ourselves.

Because many of these products are not offered in mainstream supermarkets (where additives, pesticides, preservatives and fillers reign) it can be intimidating when first learning about them. Discovering new foods (and learning to cook in general) is not only extremely exciting, but also opens us to learning about nutrition. The old adage is true. We really are what we eat. What we put into our bodies absolutely has an effect on how we feel. But, these are things you will learn as you begin exploring. So have fun, take an adventure and learn more about what you eat.

GENERAL TERMS. . .

Organic—A general term for a way food is produced. Organic farming is about sustainable agriculture.
It is sustainable in that organic farming practices replenish soil fertility without the use of synthetic pesticides and fertilizers. Organic foods also contain no artificial ingredients, preservatives and are not irradiated.

Macrobiotic—The words *macro,* meaning great, and *bio,* meaning life, are the central focus behind this dietary principle. It is more than a diet, but rather is a way of life. It is a conscious way of living in harmony with the natural order of the universe. This philosophy considers relationships between nutrients, energy flow, food quality, ancestral background, environmental and work influences, general personal health and spiritual direction. These factors weigh heavily with the selection, preparation and manner of cooking and eating, as well as the orientation of consciousness.

Vegetarian—A diet consisting of plant foods, though there are varying degrees of this. The basic vegetarian diet includes vegetables, fruits, grains, legumes, soy products, nuts, seeds, and various seasonings of herbs, spices, sauces and pastes. An ovo-lacto vegetarian eats the above foods as well as eggs and dairy products. A lacto vegetarian consumes dairy products, but no eggs. A vegan diet consists of no animal products whatsoever, including eggs, dairy and sometimes honey.

HERBS AND SPICES

Chamomile—One of the most widely used herb teas, often used for its calming properties.

Coriander—This powder is used in many spice mixtures, curries, etc. Coriander comes from cilantro.

Cumin—Comes in white or black seeds and in whole or powdered form. Used for flavoring, cumin is delicious with beans!

Eucalyptus—Native to Australia, eucalyptus contains essential oils used in herbal medicine. It is a natural antiseptic and helps tremendously with respiratory problems.

Fennel—Similar in taste and appearance to anise seeds, but usually larger, plumper and milder.

Garam masala—An aromatic combination of spices which can be made at home. Spices usually consist of cumin, cloves, coriander, black peppercorns, cinnamon, nutmeg and cardamom, but by no means is this a standard mixture. Try creating your own!

Lemon grass—A perennial plant used as a source of lemon flavor in Asian cooking. This can be found fresh or dried, though dried is usually easier to buy.

Mustard seeds—Small, redish brown, round seeds. Cooked in oil, they have a nutty flavor.

Sage—A pungent and unmistakable seasoning, used ground in a variety of dishes.

Turmeric—A root spice that provides a yellow color. It is used for pungent flavor and coloring in Indian dishes such as curries.

PRODUCE

Bok choy—A leafy green and white vegetable originating from China. It can be found fresh in oriental or international markets, or in health food stores. Tastes great in stir-fries!

Garlic—This "cure-all" is a known antibiotic cleanser and a home remedy in many cultures. The segments, known as cloves, are used in all types of cooking. Garlic also comes in a powdered form. With all these wonderful attributes, it prompts the question. . . How can you not accept garlic into your life? Eat lots!

Kale—A leafy green which is rich in vitamin C and calcium. It is a very hardy winter plant and is also inexpensive.

Okra—A delicious green vegetable, it is the principal ingredient in making gumbo. It also has a slimy texture when cooked.

Shiitake mushrooms—A gourmet mushroom used fresh or dried in soups, stews and also for medicinal purposes.

Sprouts—Consuming the sprouts of seeds or legumes is an economical way to obtain nutritious food year-round. Sprouts are best eaten raw in salads, sandwiches or in cooked vegetable dishes. Sprouting your own seeds or beans is very easy. For more information, consult your local natural food store. Some common seed and bean sprouts come from alfalfa seeds, barley, chickpeas, oats, radish, sunflowers, mung bean, peas, soybeans, sunflower seeds, wheat, lentils and Chinese red beans.

GRAINS

Barley—Has a sweet, chewy texture. Can be substituted for brown rice. Wonderful cooked for breakfast!

Bulgur—A form of whole wheat which has been cracked, partially boiled and dried. This nutty tasting, fluffy texture grain takes a very short amount of time to prepare.

Millet—A small, round, yellow grain. It is fluffier and cooks faster than rice.

Quinoa—This small, hearty grain was a staple grain of the Incas. It is a complete protein and is a source of calcium, phosphorus, iron, B vitamins and vitamin E. When cooked, it is granular and has a nutty taste. It is often used in casseroles with vegetables or in place of rice.

LEGUMES

Chickpeas—A medium-size, round, tan bean with a firm texture and absolutely delicious flavor. Popular in Middle Eastern and Mediterranean cooking.

Fava beans—Large, flat kidney-shaped bean. Light brown, strong, almost bitter taste and granular texture. Popular in the Middle East and Italy.

Lentil beans—These are small, disk-shaped beans. They can be yellow, green, red or brown. They have a delicate, creamy texture.

A WORLD OF SOY PRODUCTS

Miso—A rich, fermented soybean paste made with white rice, brown rice, corn or barley. It comes pasteurized and in several varieties from sweet white to dark red. A soybean product, it is related to tamari. Miso has a sweet taste and a salty flavor.

Soybeans—A round, pea-shaped bean that is native to Central China. It can be yellow, green, brown or black. It has a nutty flavor and firm texture. It is most commonly used to make tofu, miso, tamari and a plethora of other products.

Soy flour—Flour made from soybeans.

Tamari—A dark soy sauce made by a long, natural fermentation process.

Tempeh—A traditional Southeast Asian fermented soy product made with split soybeans, water and special bacteria. High in protein, it can be added to everything!

Tofu—A soft, bland, white block of bean curd. It is high in protein, versatile and inexpensive. Tofu can be made into dressings, dips, spreads, sauces, used in stir-fries, soups and desserts. It comes in varying degrees of hardness. Soft tofu is used for mashing, blending, desserts, etc. The firm is great for stir-fries.

TVP—(Texturized Vegetable Protein)—Made from soybeans, TVP is an excellent replacement for meat in dishes, or is wonderful to create a dish around. Found in health food stores, TVP comes in granules, flakes, chunks and 1-to-2-inch-long slices. Generally, one cup of boiling water is needed to cook (or rehydrate) one cup of TVP. Water can easily be replaced by soup stock. (Try Carla's Sumptuous Soup Stock Recipe—page 4—for a great recipe!) Once rehydrated, TVP should be refrigerated.

MISCELLANEOUS

Apple butter—A mixture of apples and sugar, cooked over a low heat. This mixture can also be bought at a health food store.

Braag—A product which is advertised as "Liquid Amino acids." Braag is naturally salty and contains all the essential amino acids. This all-purpose seasoning tastes similar to soy sauce and tamari and can be used in the same way.

Chapatis—This round, flat bread is eaten throughout India and is part of many vegetarian meals. It is made from ground flour at home or bought in a natural food store. Consult a good Indian cookbook for a recipe.

Cinnamon stick—Used for flavor and aroma, but not meant to be eaten.

Coconut milk—This milk is made by grating coconut, mixing it with water and then squeezing out the juice. It is a wonderfully thick, rich cooking base found canned in stores. Buy unsweetened coconut milk for cooking.

Ghee—Clarified butter is an oil that is semi-liquid at room temperature. It is used extensively in Indian cooking, and also as a base in making herbal salves and oils. Ghee can be bought in stores or made at home by heating butter in a specific way.

Green tea—A delicate, fragrant tea. . . found in bulk at health food stores or in tea bags.

Hemp seeds—Hemp plants are used for their fiber, seed and oil. Hemp seeds contain a great deal of protein (second to soybeans for protein content, they contain the minimum daily requirement for adults) and all eight essential amino acids. They taste great and can enhance any recipe.

Rice noodles—An inexpensive rice product used in Asian cooking. It can be found in international markets or health food stores.

Seitan—A whole wheat product cooked in soy sauce, kombu and water. Seitan (pronounced say-tan) can be used in stews, grain burgers, barbecued (great with barbecue sauce. . . mmm). Seitan has an exuberant, chewy, meatlike taste. It is also referred to as wheat gluten and wheat meat.

Soba noodles—A spaghetti shaped noodle combining buckwheat or buckwheat flour with wheat or whole wheat flour.

Sunflower seed butter—A paste made from sunflower seeds. Found in natural food stores.